Neil O'Brien was born on 10 May 1934. He completed his Master of Arts in English Literature from Calcutta University, and went on to teach English at St Xavier's College. In 1964, he joined Oxford University Press, India, where he worked for thirty-eight years and went on to become the Managing Director. He was the Chairman of the Council for the Indian School Certificate Examinations (ISC/ICSE) from 1993 to 2010, and a three-time nominated Member of Legislative Assembly in West Bengal and a Member of Parliament. He was a leader of the Anglo-Indian community, the president-in-chief of the All-India Anglo-Indian Association and headed the Frank Anthony group of schools. Popularly known as the Father of Quizzing in India, he pioneered open quizzes when he conducted the first one in 1967, in Calcutta. He was married to Joyce O'Brien and had three sons—Derek, Andy and Barry.

Neil O'Brien passed away in Calcutta on 24 June 2016.

THE CALCULTTA QUIZ BOOK

NEIL O'BRIEN

Published by
Rupa Publications India Pvt. Ltd 2017
7/16, Ansari Road, Daryaganj
New Delhi 110002

Sales Centres:
Allahabad Bengaluru Chennai
Hyderabad Jaipur Kathmandu
Kolkata Mumbai

'The Man Who Knew Everything' by Ashok Malik was first published in *The Anglo-Indian Way* (Rupa); 'More Than a Quizmaster' by Keith Flory first published in *The Statesman*, 29 June 2016; 'Neil O'Brien, the Tallest of Them All' by Devangshu Dutta first published in *Scroll.in*, 26 June 2016; 'The General of Knowledge' by Shovon Chowdhury first published in *The Indian Express*, 3 July 2016; 'The Joy of Living' by John Mason first published in *The Times of India*, 25 June 2016

ISBN: 978-81-291-3664-0

First impression 2017

10 9 8 7 6 5 4 3 2 1

Contents

The Man Who Knew Everything

Ashok Malik

'Who or what is thurifer?'

It's been some forty years since the quizmaster asked the question but Jug Suraiya, journalist, writer and, in an age and a Calcutta gone by, an avid quizzer, can remember it as if it were yesterday.

It was clear soon enough that nobody had the answer. The expressions on the teams' faces told the story. It was then that the participants and the audience, and most acutely Jug, saw a virtuoso performance. Neil O'Brien attempted to fudge the answer.

To a practised quizzer, fudging is not an artifice; it is an art form. It is to start the process of answering a question with a clue, a ghost of a clue or sometimes not even that and to negotiate with and draw out information from the quizmaster that leads him to give the game away. No one did it better than Neil O'Brien.

'Neil began waving his hands,' Jug remembers, 'as if he were performing some intricate dance mudras. "A thurifer," he said, "is a is a is a…"'

'Is a?' The quizmaster was getting impatient.

'In religious ceremonies…' Neil mumbled.

'What about religious ceremonies?' The quizmaster stopped in his tracks. Neil had him captive. The first round had been won.

'In Christian religious ceremonies,' Neil continued, doing nothing more than giving himself time, and watching the quizmaster's face as if to decode it.

'Go on,' went the quizmaster, by now confused if Neil knew the answer or whether he should put a stop to this and move to the next team.

'You know the thing with incense.'

'The thing?' The quizmaster was about to pass, but for one transfixing moment Neil looked him in the eye. Then came the flourish. With a masterful wave of his hands Neil O'Brien had the answer: 'Not "thing". He. It's the person, the person who carries the incense during worship in church.'

The quizmaster nodded, Neil and his team had the point. Jug was left not just impressed but bewildered. It was almost magical; Neil had plucked an answer out of thin air.

Later the two friends got talking. Neil confessed he had known nothing of the definition of 'thurifer'. Shortly after the question was asked, he vaguely remembered the vessel used to burn incense in church was called a thurible. Could the two words be linked? He had started off with just that surmise, finally getting his answer when the quizmaster emphasized the word 'thing', indicating, to the watchful, that he was seeking not an object but an animate being.

Jug counts Neil as among his closest and oldest friends. To him, that episode, that fudging expedition at a quiz and that answer remain emblematic of Neil. 'He is a man of erudition,' Jug would say fondly, 'but also practical common sense, and the ability to make connections.' He had the empathy, Jug says, to read clues offered in the expressions or mannerisms of another human being. Above all, he was a hard customer, a keen competitor who would fight for that answer and that point till the very end, even resorting to some intellectual gamesmanship, if necessary.

Jug Suraiya's anecdote about Neil or Neil Aloysius O'Brien to give him his full name, reflects the mosaic that made up the man. His quest to learn, to study, to seek the frontiers of knowledge; his determination to reach the identifiable goals of a successful career; his competitive edge, the result of childhood insecurities perhaps, that sublimated themselves in the most agreeable of battlegrounds, the quiz: this was at once a simple and a complex man.

Maybe he represented his rich and mixed ancestry. It would have confused a lesser person, but for Neil it was a matter of honour and a badge of pride. 'I'm Anglo-Indian,' he often said, 'as proud of the Anglo or European side of my heritage as the Indian side.'

There was somewhere in him a bit of the hardy, adventurous Thomas O'Brien, an Irish soldier who came to India shortly after the Mutiny, fought and won a medal in the Bhutan War of 1864–65 and never went home. There was also somewhere in Neil more than a bit of Nellie Bella O'Brien, his upstanding and redoubtable grandmother, born to a Bengali Christian family, married to Thomas' son Daniel in 1904 when the bride was fifteen, and the groom in his thirties and widowed early. Left to bring up her children, Nellie first educated herself becoming among Bengal's earliest women doctors and then her children. Her greatest, most rewarding mission was nurturing her grandson, Neil, who was left in her care after his parents separated in the 1940s.

Nellie left a deep impact on Neil. The medal she won at Calcutta Medical College is still one of his prized possessions. He was born to Edna and Amos in 1934, being delivered at home by his grandmother. This was around the time Nellie gave up her job in a Jalpaiguri hospital to return to Calcutta and set up a private practice. They didn't know it then, but it was to forge a bond between grandmother and grandson that only grew stronger as the years passed.

When World War II broke out, there were fears of a Japanese invasion or bombing of Calcutta. Neil and his grandmother were sent off in 1940 and then 1942 to Peshawar, where Amos' brother Patrick was a civil servant. It was in Calcutta, however, that Neil walked down the road of formal education, beginning with Loreto Convent in Sealdah that still took boys back then before moving in class 2 to St Xavier's, so close to his first home on Park Lane, just off Park Street. Soon he was living in the Jamir Lane house that is still the O'Brien home. His father had left to teach at a college in Kerala and it was Nellie who brought up little Neil. Amos subsequently became the first Christian to serve as head of the Department of English, Banaras Hindu University, and also taught at Cuttack's Ravenshaw College.

By his own admission, Neil was a shy and lonely boy. At St Xavier's, it was a Belgian Jesuit, Father John Biot, who drew him out of his shell. 'He touched my life,' Neil said, expressing an emotion that, despite the length of time, could not hide the gratitude. "I began to open up. He got me interested in sports, football, hockey and dramatics. The Kendals came to

Calcutta and performed at Xavier's. I saw every single play. My exposure to Shakespeare was not through books but because I saw the plays being performed.'

This was the trigger the inquisitive and intellectually agile lad needed. Neil was academically proficient. Those who marvel at his ability to identify and decipher obscure Latin phrases, attributes that have served him in several quizzes, would be interested to know he studied and topped Latin in school. 'It helped me with my knowledge of and curiosity for the English language,' he said. Higher education was a natural progression. Neil hopped across to St Xavier's College, exploring the world of music and theatre, becoming sociable.

In the 1950s, jobs were reserved for Anglo-Indians in government departments that had a tradition of service by the community—the Railways, the Customs and Calcutta Police. After school and certainly after college, many of Neil's Anglo-Indian friends took up jobs. 'I was envious of them and their uniforms and motorcycles,' he admitted, 'but I plodded along for an MA.' Encouraged by his grandmother, who saw academic potential in him, he went to Calcutta University, saw a different side to his city and society, and even got elected class representative in Students' Union elections.

It was in his final year as an MA student that Neil had two life-altering experiences. First, at a party at a common friend's house on Theatre Road, he met Joyce. 'It was love at first sight.' After all these years, he remains as definitive as ever. Joyce was the antithesis of Neil. Cheerful, gregarious and extroverted, she was born to a large happy Railway family of ten children. She had lived all over India in modern Maharashtra and Andhra Pradesh, Bihar and Bengal. On a family holiday years later, the O'Briens were driving from Calcutta to Madras (Kolkata to Chennai in today's parlance) when she stunned village folk at the Orissa-Andhra border by addressing them in Telugu.

Neil's and Joyce's personalities complemented each other. As they went their separate ways that evening after the party, they promised to stay in touch. Pretty soon, it was clear they were serious about each other. Joyce moved to Calcutta to her uncle's house and began teaching at South Point School. In 1959, at Christ the King Church, the two were married.

Before that, Neil had found his calling—publishing. In 1956, he joined Longman as a trainee. 'In the morning, I edited,' he says of his early days at work, 'and in the afternoons, I was taken on sales calls, to the warehouse and other departments. It was a thorough grounding in all aspects of the publishing business. Only after two years did I get an executive post.'

It was not an easy life. To supplement his income, Neil took tuitions in the evening and taught English and commercial correspondence to B.Com students at St Xavier's between 6 a.m. and 8 a.m. 'Often I'd be home only for dinner,' he said, 'it was tough but it was also strange to see that among my students were friends who had joined the Customs straight after school. They had now come back because they needed a college degree to get promoted.' By 1961, the job quotas had gone as well. Neil's focus on education had paid off.

In 1965, Neil joined Oxford University Press (OUP) as manager of its Calcutta office. He did a stint in New Delhi in the 1970s, before returning to Calcutta. In the 1990s, he went back to the capital, retiring as Managing Director of OUP in 1996. Anglo-Indians have made it to the top of the armed forces, but Neil was perhaps the first from the community to head a major private sector company. Indeed, many would see in him the very model for a young Anglo-Indian.

Even so, in the forty years he spent in publishing, Neil saw many Anglo-Indians leave India for Britain, Canada, America and Australia. It was often an instinctive and emotional decision, rather than based on a thought-out economic strategy. 'I think they got overwhelmed by the idea of having to work for "Indians",' Neil said, obviously regretful. 'I know two brothers, one of them stayed on and became a successful police officer. The other was a former army man and perhaps better qualified, but he left. And lived in oblivion in England. He gave up a comfortable life in India for almost nothing.'

It was not an option Neil even thought of exercising. 'I never considered leaving. I had to fit into the new India, I was determined. In Jamir Lane, I began to learn the language of my neighbours without studying it formally. I wanted to be a local boy.' In part this was his grandmother's influence. In part it was Joyce's influence; with her pan-Indian background, in terms of where she'd stayed, this was the only country she could call home.

Writing and publishing, education, a thirst for knowledge and learning, quizzing, public service: each of Neil's sons has inherited and optimised a facet of his father. The unit has been held together, however, by the remarkably non-judgemental Joyce—the sheet anchor of the family.

Joyce and Neil grew up and grew old together. They saw the world together, including during an unforgettable round-the-world trip that was Neil's farewell gift from OUP.

An early overseas visit took place in 1966, when OUP summoned Neil for six weeks in England and at a business event in Germany. The young couple, familiar with many of the cultural reference points of London (which self-respecting Calcuttan of that era wasn't!) had a ball. They watched theatre and sport, and television. Something caught Neil's eye: the quiz shows. 'We saw many quizzes on television,' he recalled, 'and I was hooked. It struck me that participants of Indian ethnicity, and there were a few even back then, seemed to have the answers.'

In December 1967, Neil conducted the first open quiz at the Parish Club, adjoining Christ the King Church. 'A former president had died and we wanted to organise an event in his honour,' he said. 'I suggested a quiz.' There were only five teams, but a snowball had started rolling. In the years to follow, Neil's stewardship of the Dalhousie Institute A or DI (A) team made it one of the most formidable quartets on Calcutta's open quiz circuit. It led to younger and sometimes awestruck quizzers giving him the sobriquet 'The Man Who Knows Everything'.

Ten years later, Neil began taking part in a Question Hour of quite another kind, in the West Bengal legislative assembly. Far away from politics, and even community politics, he was astounded when he called home one day from his hotel in Madras (Chennai). His flight had been delayed and he didn't want Joyce to worry. She said some of his friends had been asking for him and Jyoti Basu, newly-elected chief minister of the state, wanted to meet him. Basu, a fellow Xaverian, had sought out Neil and wanted him to accept nomination as

Anglo-Indian MLA.

Initially hesitant, Neil took to his quasi-political office with his trademark honesty of purpose. Since he held a full-time job, any advance in his community leadership role was possible only if Joyce took half the burden. She did so willingly and became actively involved in the Anglo-Indian Association, making herself a bridge between the community and its MLA.

Neil, who was to serve three terms before stepping down in 1991, realized he needed to talk to ordinary folk in the community, not just his friends, much more often and with much more patience. 'Every Monday, Wednesday and Friday,' he says, 'after work at OUP, I would go to St Mary's on Ripon Street and just sit there and meet people. They poured in, with problems of marriages, police cases, landlord evictions. I saw Anglo-Indians at their best, and I saw them at their worst.'

It was only a matter of time before Neil began to be spoken of as a prospective Anglo-Indian MP (two members of the community are nominated to the Lok Sabha or Lower House of India's Parliament). In 1991, the lawyer Frank Anthony, a long-standing MP and doyen of the community, sounded him out for the position. 'I sought permission from OUP, but they said no,' Neil explained. Unwilling to give up his chance to head OUP in India, and reach the peak of his professional career, Neil turned down the offer. In 1997, shortly after he retired from the company, Indrajit Gupta, an old friend and then India's home minister, asked Neil again. This time he was ready.

In the interim, in 1993, Frank Anthony had died and Neil had donned his mantle as senior statesman of the

Anglo-Indian community. Just after Frank Anthony's death, Neil took his place as Chairman of the Council for the Indian School Certificate Examinations. This completed the circle and brought him back to the academic domain that had reared him. He stepped down from his leadership of the Council in 2010, insisting it was time to retire and play with the grandchildren.

It wasn't a quiet retirement, though. Neil was too much of a workaholic and too full of energy to settle into simply doing nothing. To the end, he remained a very involved, very hands-on president-in-chief of the All-India Anglo-Indian Association, as well as president of the All-India Anglo-Indian Education Institution, which runs the three Frank Anthony Public Schools. This was appropriate as the community and the cause of education had been his principal motivations.

The sense of curiosity never left him either, nor the sheer excitement of life. In 2016, frail and ailing, his body having all but given up but his brain still agile as ever, he listened to old songs and watched a Muhammad Ali film (Neil was a lifelong boxing fan) from his hospital bed. The questions never stopped. 'What's the latest?' to the friend on the phone. 'So what next? What's the plan?' to his sons, all of them trapped between sorrow and amazement as they realized the spirit was willing but the flesh was weak, and time was slipping by.

When the clock stopped, as it must for all of us, there was sadness of course, but also a bunch of happy thoughts and memories of a rich life, well lived, of that marvelous mind, that voice, at once stentorian and compassionate, that impish smile. Who knows, he may well have been setting a quiz for the angels.

AcademiCAL

(Education)

1. Who was the first principal of Sanskrit College?

2. Which institution was shifted from Chowringhee to Sans Souci Theatre in January 1860?

3. Who refused to accept his salary, which was half the pay the Europeans received for the position of Professor of Physics in Presidency College, and went without it for three years as a form of protest?

4. Which is the first co-educational school in Calcutta to be affiliated to the West Bengal Board of Secondary Education?

5. Who was the first proprietor of Calcutta Public Library, which was established in 1836?

6. Which institution was originally known as 'General Assembly's Institution'?

7. In 1831, who was accused of irreverence by the orthodox Hindu parents of his students and forced to resign as a faculty member from the Hindu College?

8. Who designed the logo of the Patha Bhavan school, founded on 28 June 1965?

9. Which school, founded in 1789 for the English community of Calcutta, is believed to be the oldest English-medium school in Kolkata?

10. Which educationist was the Speaker of the West Bengal Assembly from 1952 to 1958?

11. Begum Rokeya opened a school in a small house on

Waliullah Lane with only a few students. Later, it was taken over by the Government of West Bengal. How do we know this reputed school today?

12. Who, along with Judoo Nath Bose, was the first graduate of Calcutta University?

13. '*Satyam Shivam Sundaram*' is the motto of which school, founded in 1952 by Mrs Rukmini Devi Birla?

14. What is the Bengali word for statistics, coined by Rabindranath Tagore?

15. Who joined Calcutta Medical College as its first Indian lady student and later became one of the first practising lady doctors in India?

16. Established in 1879, which is the first woman's college of India?

17. The first women's college to be sponsored by the government is named after the famous wife of Sri Chittaranjan Das. Name her.

18. On 10 January 1842, which school opened in a building on Middleton Row that was formerly occupied by Henry Vansittart, Governor of Bengal (1760–64) and Sir Elijah Impey, first Chief Justice of the Supreme Court at Calcutta?

19. After whom was the West Bengal University of Technology renamed?

20. Which institution, established in 1836, is named after a

Frenchman who came to India as a private in the armies of the East India Company, in 1752?

21. In which school did Mother Teresa teach before starting Missionaries of Charity?

22. After which famous person is the library at IIM-Calcutta named?

23. Which institution was founded by Mr Astvatsatur Muradkhanian and Mr Manatsakan Vardanian in 1821?

24. Which Nobel Laureate gave Amartya Sen his name?

25. Who became the first Indian Vice-Chancellor of the University of Calcutta?

AesthetiCAL

The Arts

1. In which landmark in Kolkata would you find the largest oil painting in India, painted by Veretchagin?

2. In Bengali fiction, who wrote *Vancouver-er Vampire*, *Honduras-e Hahakar* and *Atlantic-er Atanka*?

3. Which legendary magician died in Hokkaido, Japan, in 1971, during a tour showcasing his *Indrajaal*?

4. Which novel, set in a hotel named Shahjahan, revolves around the lives of Sata Bose, Marco Polo and Karabi Guha?

5. Who wrote the English poem 'The Child', which was inspired by a play the poet had seen in Oberammergau near Munich?

6. Who designed the original cover of Bibhutibhushan Bandopadhyay's *Chander Pahar*?

7. Which detective has a son named Boomboom and a niece named Tupur who helps her in investigations?

8. Which famous author wrote works under the pen name 'Kalkut' meaning 'poison'?

9. Which literary character introduced in the story 'Satyanweshi' has a wife named Satyavati?

10. Who wrote these books on art: *Banglar Brata*, *Bharatshilpe Murti* and *Bharatshilper Sadanga*?

11. What is the name of the slum in Dominique Lapierre's *The City of Joy*?

12. Who translated a part of Homer's Iliad in his book *Hector Badh*?

13. How do we popularly know the famous Bengali writer Prabodh Kumar Bandopadhyay?

14. Which famous artist, born on 11 April 1887, often used the calligraphic brush lines of Kalighat patuas in his works?

15. In the poem 'Banalata Sen', Jibanananda Das compared her eyes with… ?

16. Who wrote the English novel *Rajmohan's Wife*, which appeared serially in *Indian Field* in 1864?

17. Who was known as 'Kantakobi' in West Bengal?

18. A story by which English cricket captain, nicknamed Cockroach, was published in the book *The Weekenders: Adventures in Calcutta*?

19. In which novel by Jhumpa Lahiri would you meet the brothers, Subhash and Udayan, raised in Tollygunge, Kolkata?

20. 'To Calcutta, much abused, much loved and always interesting'. Who dedicated one of his books on Calcutta with this line as part of the preface?

21. What are the massive sculptures made by Ramkinkar Baij, now installed at the main entrance to the Reserve Bank office in New Delhi, called?

22. *The Calcutta Chromosome*, by Amitav Ghosh, is based on

the life and times of which scientist?

23. Between 1897 and 1912, who had contributed the articles, 'The theory of half-tone dot', 'The 60 degree Crossline screen' and 'Multiple Stops' to the *Penrose Annual*?

24. Which art form, introduced by Abanindranath Tagore, is being used to train 'Green Engineers' at IIT Kharagpur?

25. Who altered the 'Bombai Dastur' style of draping a saree to create Thakurbarir sari, which became the archetype for the Bengali way of wearing it?

CinematiCAL

Films

1. Which was Satyajit Ray's first colour film based on his original screenplay?

2. Who won the award for Best Director at the 62nd National Film Awards?

3. *Calcutta 71*, a film by Mrinal Sen, comprised the stories of three Bengali writers. Who were they?

4. Where was Chitrabani, founded by Fr Gaston Roberge, first established?

5. The American animated television series *The Simpsons* created which character to pay homage to Satyajit Ray?

6. Which 1937 film is said to be the first film to use songs by Rabindranath Tagore?

7. Who produced the Uttam–Suchitra starrer *Saptapadi* (1961)?

8. Which nine-letter word, relating to the film industry based in Kolkata, is said to have been popularised by a sound technician named Wilford E. Deming?

9. *The Last Lear* was the first English language film of which director?

10. In which of his own films did Ritwik Ghatak play the role of Nilkantha Bagchi, an alcoholic intellectual?

11. Which famous director was the cinematographer in Aparna Sen's film *Mr and Mrs Iyer*?

12. Who directed *The Legend of Fat Mama*, a documentary

centering around the Chinese community of Calcutta?

13. With which film did Aparna Sen make her directorial debut?
14. In 1931, who directed the film version of Rabindranath Tagore's dance drama *Natir Puja* at B.N. Sircar's request?
15. Who narrated the story in Mrinal Sen's 1969 film *Bhuvan Shome*?
16. Who was the first winner of the National Award for Best Actor?
17. What was the occupation of Hazari Pal, the character played by Om Puri in *City of Joy*?
18. Who was elected from the Ghatal constituency in the 2014 General Elections?
19. Which famous actor's mother Sunetra Ghatak is related to Ritwik Ghatak?
20. For which film did Mithun Chakraborty receive the National Award for Best Actor in 1992?
21. Which address is the name of a 2005 film directed by Aparna Sen?
22. Which actor directed the 1982 film *An August Requiem*?
23. Who received the Dadasaheb Phalke award for 2011?
24. Who pedalled across the streets of Kolkata in a pink kurta in the 2015 film *Piku*?

25. Which French director came to Kolkata to shoot his film *The River* and was accompanied by Satyajit Ray on his trips in search of locations?

ComiCAL

The Lighter Side

1. Fill in the blank to complete this line from a poem by Sukumar Ray: *Ramgorurer chhana,*____*taader maana.*

2. In which film does Utpal Dutt call Santosh Dutta '*Gobeshok Gobochondro Gyanotirtho Gyanorotno Gyanambudhi Gyanochuramoni*'?

3. From which film is the song '*Shing Nei Tobu Naam Tar Shingho*', sung by Kishore Kumar?

4. In which 2012 film, directed by Anik Dutta, does a group of spirits try to save its resting place from being brought down by dishonest builders?

5. According to a poem by Sukumar Ray, what belonging to '*head office er boro babu*' goes missing?

6. Which actor, famous for his comic roles in Satyajit Ray films, started the theatre group Chalachal?

7. In the novel *Charmurti* by Narayan Gangopadhyay, who is the third accomplice of Teni da, besides Habul and Pyalaram?

8. Colloquially, what is an Italian salon?

9. Gopal Bhaar is a one of the Navratnas in the court of which king?

10. In 1969, who created the comic-strip characters Nonte and Phonte for *Kishore Bharati* magazine?

11. In the 19th century rhyme '*Jaat marle tin Seney*' (Caste has been destroyed by the three Sens), who were the three 'Sens'?

12. *Shwet Pathorer Table, Lotakambal, Rakhish Ma Rosheboshey* are famous works by which author?

13. Finish the popular saying: *Laage taaka debe* _______ *Sen.*

14. The comic-strip superhero Batul the Great is based on which famous bodybuilder?

15. Complete the rhyme: *Baghbazar's Nobin Das, Rosogolla's …*

16. What are offsprings of parents, one from East Bengal and the other from West Bengal, colloquially called?

17. Which poet, while living in Government House in Kolkata, complained, 'No rest in Husstlefussabad'?

18. Which Kolkata-born filmmaker directed the popular films *Chupke Chupke, Khoobsurat* and *Golmaal*?

19. In which film, revolving around Annapurna Boarding House, do Suchitra Sen and Uttam Kumar play the roles of Romola and Rampriti?

20. What are the names of the two fictional timber merchant brothers created by Shibram Chakraborty?

21. In which Uttam Kumar film would you come across the song '*Ami ekjon shantoshishto potninishto bhadrolok*'?

22. *Hutom Pyanchar Naksha* is a compilation of satirical sketches by which author?

23. Cricket balls in the city are often referred to as 'deuce balls'. Why?

24. What is the local Anglo-Indian term for what is called a 'band party'?

25. Who is the lead vocalist of the music band Bandage?

More Than a Quizmaster

Keith Flory

It required much moral courage to issue an exhortation to 'look forward not backwards' to the Anglo-Indian community that has such an overdose of nostalgia flavouring its lifeblood, but Neil O'Brien was richly endowed with precisely that quality.

It is, in some ways, a pity that most of the media accounts following his death on 24 June 2016 focused on his pioneering role as a quizmaster: he certainly was that par excellence, but there was so much more to that legendary figure. Overuse has taken the edge off the 'icon' accolade, yet O'Brien can be described in no better term for a personal brilliance that bloomed in the fields of publishing, education and community leadership. Like all true giants he cannot be 'slotted'.

Having made his mark in the post-colonial era, O'Brien was not weighed down with historical baggage, and that reinforced his belief that members of his community could make it to the top in any field of their choice. Thus he looked beyond the Railways, Police and Armed Forces when selecting people for community awards, reaching out to designers, hair-stylists, apparel-producers. Not that he decried 'traditional' professions such as teaching or nursing, just that the visionary in him wanted an expansion of horizons. That visionary quality was manifest in a very different manner in his stewardship of the chain of Frank Anthony Public Schools: new auditoriums, laboratories and classrooms were added. Associated with schools in so many cities, he always laid emphasis on the 'three Ls—libraries, laboratories and loos'. He had that eye for detail, modifying the oaths taken by prefects, etc. He was a perfectionist in everything he did, and he did a lot. Like all those who seek to take his people on a new path, O'Brien did ruffle feathers.

A section of the community accused him of not doing enough for the weaker sections, but his priority was teaching a man to catch fish rather than providing one. Not for him the easy route to get the expats to fill a begging bowl, a policy that saw him being accused of arrogance and indifference.

He firmly refused to confuse popularity with populism. O'Brien was a 'modern' who wanted the 'local' dimension of his community to be recognized as much as its European. Not surprisingly, he passed on to his family his fluency in the Bengali language and culture. He knew where the future of his people lay, and did not want them imprisoned by 'history'. To list his many accomplishments would be a tall order, but there must be no overlooking his contribution to the City of Joy.

Though many facets of his unique personality earned him nationwide appreciation, he privately relished being dubbed 'Neil O'Brien of Calcutta', for whom Park Street, St Xavier's, the Dalhousie Institute and the Church of Christ the King were the holy of holies.

Neil passed away in Calcutta in June 2016. He did not favour his grave being adorned with flowers, so the abundant floral tributes received were spread over the graves in the vicinity as if all the residents of the Lower Circular Road cemetery were welcoming a special arrival.

EconomiCAL

Business

1. Before Independence, which brand advertised itself as 'Entirely Indian—Indian capital, Indian labour, Indian materials and Indian brain'?

2. Which company launched the first branded Chyawanprash in India?

3. Founded in 1919, which was the first company of the Birla Industrial Conglomerate?

4. Which Indian industrialist's statue would you find on the eastern side of the Victoria Memorial garden?

5. Which company has its headquarters in 'Virginia House'?

6. In the mid 1950s, the Calcutta Electrical Manufacturing Company became a part of the CK Birla Group and later renamed…

7, Lyons Range, Calcutta, constructed in 1928, houses which organization?

8. Who got a senior British military officer's dress tailored by Calcutta-based British firm, Harman's, for the annual session of the Indian National Congress in 1928 in Calcutta?

9. Whose business card read: 'The fruit of silence is prayer; The fruit of prayer is faith; The fruit of faith is love; The fruit of love is service; and The fruit of service is peace'?

10. 33 Syed Amir Ali Avenue is a famous address in Kolkata. It is the location of…

11. In 1947, Debu Barick changed the name of the popular

eatery Dipti Cabin to...

12. Which animal appears on the logo of Boroline, a brand established by Gourmohon Dutta of Calcutta?
13. In 1822, who founded the Oriental Life Assurance Society, along with three commercial houses Fergusson & Co., Cruttenden & Co., and Mackintosh & Co.?
14. Which industrialist, born on 1 March 1930, was a member of the Rajya Sabha from 2000 to 2006?
15. Which organization has been looking after the maintenance of Rabindra Setu, better known as Howrah Bridge, since its commissioning in 1943?
16. Beni Madhab Seal is famous for publishing which particular book?
17. In 2014, Sourav Ganguly, Harshavardhan Neotia, Utsav Parekh and which other Calcuttan joined forces with Atlético de Madrid to form Atlético de Kolkata?
18. For the ad campaign of which soap did Rituparno Ghosh write '*Dekhte khaaraap maakhte bhaalo*'?
19. Which scientist founded Bengal Chemical & Pharmaceutical Works Limited at 91 Upper Circular Road, Calcutta?
20. Who was the first President of the Indian Chamber of Commerce in Kolkata?
21. Which newspaper was established in 1875 as an outgrowth of an earlier newspaper *The Friend of India*?

22. In 2012, a 60-rupee coin was released to mark the 60th anniversary of which enterprise in Kolkata?

23. Which group took control of Dunlop India Ltd in 2005?

24. The first job of which actor was with Shaw Wallace and later with the shipping firm Bird and Co. as a freight broker?

25. Which was the first life insurance company set up in Kolkata?

GastronomiCAL

Food

1. When Nawab Wajid Ali Shah was deposed to Metiabruz, what did his chefs add to the Awadhi biriyani, that is now an integral part of Calcuttan biriyani?

2. In Anglo-Indian homes in the city, what would you be eating if you were served 'tyre'?

3. Which popular drink did nationalist leader Prafulla Chandra Ray ask the owners of Paramount to prepare, to cool young India and fire its entrepreneurial zeal?

4. Which famous sweet in Bengal is named after Countess Charlotte Canning, wife of Governor General Charles Canning?

5. Who started the oldest Jewish bakery in Calcutta with the modest aim of serving households in and around New Market?

6. '*Nikhilesh Paris-e Moydul Dhakate, Nei tara aaj kono khobore, Grander guitarist Goanese D' Souza, ghumiye ache je aaj kobor...*' From which popular song are these lines taken?

7. The first Michelin-star restaurant in Calcutta is located in Quest Mall. Name the restaurant.

8. What name did Rabindranath Tagore give Jalajog's Lal Doi?

9. Nobin Chandra prepared which sweet for Maharani Swarnamoyee Devi (the dowager of the house of Cossimbazar) after she regretted that there were no more sweets to excite her jaded palate?

10. How did 'Breast cutlet' get its name?

11. Which food item was created by Hasan Reza, a group D employee with the civic body, to please his English bosses, who had a strong dislike for food that left oil on their hands?

12. Which restaurant, one of the oldest surviving family-owned Chinese restaurants in Kolkata, is famous for its 'chimney soup' and 'Josephine noodles'?

13. What was advertised by Dwarik Ghosh as 'sheeter sanjivani'?

14. What is the Anglo-Indian term for a 'dalpuri'?

15. What new dimension did Pragya Sundari, Rabindranath Tagore's niece, add to Bengali banquets (Bhoj Sabha)?

16. For which food item is the Golbari of Shyambazar, originally named New Punjabi Restaurant, famous?

17. In which eatery, at 40/1, Jatindra Mohan Avenue, is the prawn cutlet said to have originated?

18. The famous restaurant Bhajohori Manna is named after a Bengali song by which singer?

19. The name of which restaurant in Park Street, literally translates into 'the place of good bread'?

20. If you want to have one of the famous bread pakoras at Milan da's canteen in Jadavpur University, what should you ask for?

21. Which hotel in the city houses restaurants named The Hub, Sonargaon and Chinoiserie?

22. If you came across a vendor wearing a white kurta and Gandhi topi, what would he most probably be selling?

23. The idea of which dish, now their signature dish, was registered as a 'protected regional product' by Peter Cat?

24. According to one school of thought, the rituals surrounding the making of 'kasundi' begins on which auspicious day in the month of Baisakh?

25. Joseph and Frieda, a Swiss couple, decided to open a European style tea room in the mid 1920s. Name this establishment.

GeographiCAL

Roads

1. Which street was initially named after the deer park of Elijah Impey, the Chief Justice of the Supreme Court of Judicature at Fort William in Bengal?
2. In 2014, after which singer was Jorabagan Street renamed?
3. What does 'BT' in BT Road, starting from Shyambazar, stand for?
4. To commemorate whose 400th birth anniversary was Theatre Road renamed?
5. In 2007, which area featured as the Best Literary Treasure Hunt on *TIME'S Best of Asia List*?
6. The founder of the Bratachari Movement has a road in Calcutta named after him. Who was he?
7. On 13 September 1997, where was Mother Teresa's funeral service held?
8. In which park was the largest meeting in support of INA prisoners held in November 1945?
9. Which street was named after the Jewish father–son real estate magnates who built Chowringhee Mansions, Esplanade Mansions and the synagogue Maghen David?
10. Which present-day location used to be known as Band Stand?
11. What name was given to the village established by the United Brothers' Association to house fifty underprivileged tribal families?

12. Which poem was written by Allen Ginsberg in memory of the refugees in the camps along the main road that lead from Bangladesh to India, during the Bangladesh Liberation War?

13. Prince Anwar Shah Road in Kolkata is named after a descendant of which ruler, born in 1750?

14. In 1979, the College Square garden was named after which famous Indian?

15. The Calcutta Municipal Corporation has named the main road in Metiabruz after the last king of Awadh. Name him.

16. What is the official name of the Park Circus-Parama Island flyover?

17. In 2013, Dhakuria Bridge was renamed after which spiritual teacher?

18. After which Vietnamese President was Harrington Street renamed?

19. After which famous painter was Hungerford Street renamed?

20. Russell Street was named after Sir Henry Russell. Which important position did he hold from 1806 to 1813?

21. In 1958, whose statue was replaced by that of Mahatma Gandhi at the Chowringhee–Park Street crossing?

22. After which singer was Garcha Road renamed in 2014?

23. Where would you find Netaji's statue which was sculpted

by Nagesh Yoglekar and unveiled by the Calcutta Municipal Corporation (CMC) in 1969?

24. The Sealdah flyover has been renamed as…

25. On 1 July 1986, Doordarshan Kolkata got a new and permanent address in which area?

HistoriCAL

The Past

1. What does Belvedere House, once the winter residence of British viceroys, house today?

2. What became the subsequent family name of Panchanan and Sukdev Kushari who settled in Gobindapur?

3. What was was first sung at the 12th session of the Indian National Congress, held in Calcutta on 28 December 1896?

4. Where will you find the Burmese pagoda that was brought from Prome in Burma by Lord Dalhousie and erected in 1854?

5. Which notable landmark was constructed between 1806 and 1813 with money received from lotteries?

6. On 28 January 1882, what was opened by Major E Baring, Member of the Governor General's Council, at 7, Council House Street?

7. In 1895, who gave a public demonstration of electro-magnetic waves in Calcutta, using them to remotely ring a bell and to explode some gunpowder?

8. Who successfully defended Sri Aurobindo Ghosh in the famous Alipore Bomb Case?

9. The 'transfer' of which famous Indian is often regarded as the only known submarine-to-submarine transfer of a human during World War II?

10. Who became the first English governor of the affairs of the East India Company in Bengal?

11. Which post, created in 1720 by the British, was first occupied by Gobindaram Mitra?

12. Why was Calcutta named Alinagar?

13. Who started the first Durga Puja with an idol at Belur Math, even though as a rule this kind of ritualistic worship was not conducted there?

14. What was *The Calcutta General Advertiser* better known as?

15. In which building, locally known as Bharat Sabha, on Bowbazar Street, was *Jana Gana Mana* first sung during the annual conference of the Indian National Congress on 27 December 1911?

16. The first national flag in India is said to have been hoisted on 7 August 1906, in the Parsee Bagan Square (Green Park) in Calcutta. It had three horizontal strips of red, yellow and...

17. How is the monument, erected in 1828 to commemorate the victory of the British army under David Ochterlony over the Nepal army, popularly known?

18. Which site was originally intended as a ground to test-fire the guns of the Fort William?

19. Which paper, edited by Rabindranath Tagore, was the official organ of the Brahma Samaj?

20. Who was the first Indian to qualify for the Indian Civil Services?

21. Between 1797and 1805, which Governor General paid a lot of attention to the growth of public architecture in Calcutta that led to its description as the 'City of Palaces'?

22. Who presided over the first session of the Indian National Congress held at Bombay in 1885?

23. In 1869, Surendranath Banerjea passed the competitive examination for the Indian Civil Services but was barred from joining. Why?

24. What was regarded as the last capital city of independent Bengal before it was shifted to Calcutta by Warren Hastings?

25. Who worked as a moneylender in Calcutta and served in the Revenue Department of the East India Company from 1809 to 1814?

Neil O'Brien, the Tallest of Them All

Devangshu Dutta

I must have been around six or seven years old when I met this slim, athletic man with an upright bearing that made him look taller than he was. Uncle Neil was my classmate Andy's (Andrew Clive) dad and Aunty Joyce's husband. He was a 'Xaverian in good standing', a well-known ex-student of the Calcutta school, and a prominent member of the Anglo-Indian community. He was also a seriously good runner who routinely won the Fathers' Race at school sports days.

Some six or seven years later, I discovered quizzing. My school—St Xavier's Collegiate School, or SXCS—had just won this radio quiz show called the Bournvita Quiz Contest, which led to some of us getting interested in this mindsport. The first quiz I ever watched was held at the Grail Club, which operated out of an annexe to the Park Hotel. It was that strange Calcutta ritual known as an Open Quiz—a quiz where anybody could form teams and participate.

Our school team was participating in it. Francis Groser was the quizmaster and the team (the only one with non-adults) was doing well. Quite a few of us were in the audience and cheering the SXCS team on, in much the same fashion that we cheered the school's hockey and football teams. Groser had prepared a special round on flags as a surprise—and it so happened that one of the SXCS team members—Abhijit Banerjee—knew every flag since the time of Carthage.

The school team swept into the lead and admittedly, the support from the 'stands' got a little raucous. A prominent member of the Grail Club, whom I will refer to only as the late 'Fishface', got up and demanded that:

1. The school's supporters be evicted,
2. The school team be disqualified because of its noisy supporters, and
3. A permanent ban be placed on schools participating in genteel affairs like quizzes.

The SXCS contingent responded to Fishface in much the same way that we responded to bad refereeing in a football match.

Neil was leading the Dalhousie Institute, as he always did, when he wasn't the QM—the Quizmaster. His wife, Aunty Joyce, was in the audience, as always. She was the first person to stand up and tell Fishface that he was being absurd and unfair to the boys. Neil was the second. He also made calming noises all round in that deep voice. We subsided, Fishface left in high dudgeon, and the quiz carried on, with Aunty Joyce continuing to mutter indignantly on our behalf.

The SXCS won that quiz, mainly due to the flag round. The Dalhousie Institute came second and it was pretty clear even to a newbie that Neil was an extraordinarily good quizzer. If it hadn't been for him and Aunty Joyce on that day, it's quite possible that the SXCS would have been forced out of participation in open quizzes. (It was forced out a few years later, essentially because it embarrassed adult teams by winning. After that, the SXCS quizzed as "Xaverians".)

A year or so later, I got into the SXCS team, and experienced Neil's formidable skills as a QM for the first time. The first quiz I ever participated in was a school thing at St James, with Neil as the QM. He rarely asked 'flat' questions, which is why his quizzes were so different.

It wasn't necessarily that he dealt in the esoteric. He just framed questions differently, in a manner akin to crossword puzzle clues, tantalising quizzers with little hints and bits of information that had to be put together just so. T.S. Eliot was a bank clerk who wrote about cats; Gene Tunney was a Shakespearean scholar who boxed.

As a quizzer, he also guessed well, reversing that framing process to fudge his way to answers. It helped that he was knowledgeable about a wide range of things, ranging from sports (boxing, wrestling, poker) and movies to literature and current affairs. He also had that knack for dredging up something obscure from the back of his mind at just the right moment.

Mind you, he was hidebound when it came to formats. I remember when his eldest son, Derek (Derek Peter), started putting quizzes together with unusual formats. 'Dad' was the biggest critic. He hated gimmicks. I remember his shaking his head dismissively at a quiz where Derek told participants to shoot hoops on the basketball court. (He could shoot baskets as well as the next man, perhaps better, but he did not think quizzing and basketball practice mixed.)

He would not even consider sensible innovations like flat scoring and infinite bounce. A Neil O'Brien quiz always went the same way. You qualified for a final from a written round, you drew lots, you sat where the lots put you. Direct questions were scored at twice the rate of bonuses, an equal number of rounds went clockwise and anti-clockwise. There was a music round and a visual round.

It was a format that he had ironed out in the late 1960s and he stuck to it. Despite the format's predictable rigidity and its flaws, his trademark Dalhousie Institute Open Quiz and the few occasions where he presided over the Eddie Hyde Memorial as QM, were always among the most eagerly awaited events on the Calcutta quizzing calendar.

In-between the quizzes, I also got to know the man slightly. He was open-hearted and generous in the very best traditions of the Anglo-Indian community. Every quiz at the Dalhousie Institute must have cost him a fortune in drinks since he ended up standing a dozen people at the leaSt He often donated gift coupons from Oxford University Press (OUP), where he was the Managing Director, for quizzes when prizes were running short. In an odd way, that helped shape my literary tastes because OUP used to import Faber, which published modern classics that were otherwise unavailable.

The O'Briens kept open house. Joyce and he and, of course, the boys, spoke pitch-perfect colloquial Bengali and they interacted with pretty much everyone from the local fishmonger to the Vice Chancellor of Jadavpur University. Neil was always an interesting and entertaining conversationalist, able to find a spin on any subject under the sun.

In between the quizzes, he ran the Dalhousie Institute, and in-between running the Institute, he ran OUP. He also headed the Indian Certificate of Secondary Education (ICSE) board. He represented his community with distinction in Parliament. He was part of a time when Calcutta was still casually multicultural, with its potpourri of Jews, Armenians and Anglo-Indians. In fact, he was one of the very last anchors to my rapidly fading memories of that era.

Actually, Neil Aloysius O'Brien was even taller than he looked. Rest in Peace, Uncle Neil!

LexiCAL

Origins

1. Kumortuli
2. Baithakhana
3. Chitpur
4. Majumder
5. Creek Row
6. Baroari Puja
7. Eden Gardens
8. Tirreti Bazar
9. Writer's Bulding
10. Watgunge
11. Mukhopadhyay
12. Tangra
13. Paikpara
14. Entally
15. Shyambazar
16. Sukea Street
17. Barabazar
18. Kalutola
19. Harkara
20. Chowringhee

21. Laha
22. Kankurgachhi
23. Bonedi
24. Ultodanga
25. Khansama

LoCAL

A Mixed Bag

1. With an entry fee of 50 paise, what was inaugurated by Mrityunjay Bandyopadhyay, on 5 March 1976, on the ground opposite the Academy of Fine Arts?

2. '18, Lalbazar Street, Kolkata - 700 001' is the address of the headquarters of...

3. For contribution to which field are you most likely to receive the Golden Royal Bengal Tiger Award?

4. If you jokingly told your rickshaw to take you from Laltania to Paratha Mutton Stew, from where to where would you be going?

5. '*Aha tumi shundori koto Kolkata*' is a popular song by which singer?

6. With which fictional character from Potoldanga would you associate the phrase, 'De La Grande Mephistopheles. Yak. Yak.'?

7. Which English novelist was born in Calcutta on 18 July 1811?

8. Which was the first film to be screened by the Calcutta Film Society, founded by Satyajit Ray, Bansi Chandra Gupta and others, in 1947?

9. Which famous actor of yesteryear recited the *Mahishashur Mardini*, usually associated with Birendra Krishna Bhadra, on AIR in 1976?

10. What is the official website of Gorachand Paul and Sons, an organization of artisans?

11. In which newspaper was our National Anthem published for the first time under the title *Bharata-vidhata*?
12. What do most of the shops at the Raja Katra at Barabazar, which originally belonged to the Maharaja of Burdwan, deal in?
13. In 1924, who became the first elected mayor of the city of Calcutta?
14. The area known as Russapugla was renamed as...
15. Most shops in Radhabajar, situated behind Dalhousie Square, sell...
16. What is the English name for the flower chandramallika?
17. Which hotel was popularly called 'Wilson's Hotel' in the mid 1800s?
18. In 1943, who joined a British-run advertising agency, D.J. Keymer, as a junior visualiser, and worked there for thirteen years?
19. If Buddi girl was the name given to the oldest girl in an Anglo household, how was a young girl referred to by the domestic help?
20. To whom did the giant tortoise, 'Adwaita', a resident of the Alipore Zoo and one of longest living animals in the world, originally belong?
21. Who is the author of *Kalikata Kamalalaya*, one of the first books to have the name of the city in its title?

22. *Bhayankar Sundar* was the first adventure story to feature which fictional character?

23. Who founded the St John's Ambulance courses in first-aid and home nursing?

24. On 27 March 1902, the first electric tramcar in Calcutta ran from _____ to Kidderpore. Fill in the blank.

25. The name of the Ahiritola area comes from the word 'ahiri' meaning...

MusiCAL

Music

1. About which restaurant did Usha Uthup say, 'I am what I am today because of ____________. It is my home?'

2. Who wrote the story and composed the music for the film *Rickshawallah*?

3. Which singer/songwriter has penned the books *Chhowache Kolom* and *Shomoyer Baire* and also created a graphic novel *Antony O Chandrabindoo*?

4. Which group was set up in 1958 by singer Ruma Guha Thakurta, music composer Salil Chowdhury and director Satyajit Ray?

5. Which famous sitarist, born in Calcutta, received the Padma Shri in 1968?

6. Which music institution was established in 1915 by Dr Phillipe Sandre?

7. Which guitarist received a Grammy nomination in the Best Traditional World Music category for his 2008 solo album *Calcutta Chronicles: Indian Slide Guitar Odyssey*?

8. Which is the first Bengali band to have performed at the UN headquarters in New York?

9. The name of which music group, founded by Gautam Chattopadhyay, is said to have been borrowed from a poem by Jibanananda Das?

10. In 1996, which Bengali singer sang '*Purano shei diner kotha*' with American folk singer Pete Seeger, at Nazrul Manch?

11. '*Bagichay bulbuli tui*', considered to be the first recorded Bengali ghazal, was composed by…

12. In 1902, who became the first Indian to record on a gramophone?

13. Ramnidhi Gupta (better known as Nidhubabu) is credited with contributing which form of music to Bengal?

14. Before moving to Bollywood, Pritam was a part of which Bengali rock band whose first album was *Aar Jani Na*?

15. Which singer sang a number of songs as 'Tapan Kumar' in Calcutta?

16. He was born Probodh Chandra Dey; he won the Dadasaheb Phalke Award in 2007; his last recorded Hindi film song was for the 2006 film *Umar*. Who am I talking about?

17. Who won the National Award in 2009 for Best Male Playback Singer for his work in Suman Mukhopadhyay's film *Mahanagar@Kolkata*?

18. Who was the first person to compose the music for Bankim Chandra Chattopadhyay's *Vande Mataram*?

19. Which singer shows her love for Calcutta by wearing a bindi bearing the first letter of the alphabet of the Bengali name of the city?

20. Which musician made his acting debut in Mrinal Sen's *Chalchitra*?

21. Which famous singer, also known as Akhtari Bai Faizabadi, made a cameo appearance in Satyajit Ray's *Jalsaghar*?

22. What is the name of the Light and Sound show held at Victoria Memorial every evening?

23. Rabindranath Tagore's '*Diner Sheshe Ghumer Deshe*' was set to tune by...

24. Ustad Rashid Ali Khan collaborated with which Bengali singer for the Rabindrasangeet album *Yatra 1*?

25. Who made his Bengali film debut as a singer in Phani Burma's *Nimai Sanyasi*?

NautiCAL

Waterbodies

1. Which ghat was built in 1843 in memory of a secretary of the Asiatic Society of Bengal?

2. How did Howrah get its name?

3. Colonel Watson started the first marine yard at which place in present-day Kolkata?

4. In 2005, who became the first woman to swim across sea channels off five continents?

5. Whom does the Lascar Memorial on Strand Road commemorate?

6. After which Chief Minister of West Bengal was Salt Lake City renamed?

7. After twenty-three unsuccessful attempts, where in Calcutta was the first subsurface water tapped by drilling a borehole?

8. In 1775, an Englishman extended the distributary leading from the Hooghly river right upto east Bengal to save his wife Anna Maria any discomfort. How is this waterbody popularly known today?

9. The British renamed a settlement called Hajipur as…

10. Babu Ghat is named after the husband of which famous lady?

11. The 'Baba and Mai' monument, along the banks of river Hooghly, honours the Indian indentured workers who had migrated to…

12. Swapnapuri was a station of the toy train service that was stopped in 1990. Where was it located?

13. Which bridge, commissioned on 10 October 1992, is named after a 19th century Bengali educationist and reformer?

14. Mira Nair shot scenes for her movie *The Namesake* on the platform of which ghat?

15. After which lady is the Second Vivekananda Setu named?

16. Which is the second oldest ghat of Calcutta?

17. Which ditch was dug in 1742 to ward off raiders from the West and was partly filled up in 1799 to create Lower Circular Road?

18. Name the Japanese steamship on which a group of weary Indians reached Calcutta on 27 September 1914 after they were refused entry into Canada.

19. Who was the first Indian Port Commissioner of Calcutta?

20. King George's Dock was later renamed as…

21. The Willingdon Bridge over the Hoogly River is now known by what name?

22. Who arrived in Calcutta on 25 September 1783, aboard the frigate *Crocodile*?

23. In 1790, the first dry dock was built at which ghat?

24. The naval base in Kolkata is named after which famous personality?

25. Which hotel houses restaurants named The Bridge and The Anchorage Bar?

The General of Knowledge

Shovon Chowdhury

The Dalhousie Institute was the first club I ever entered. I was eighteen at the time. Calcutta was full of clubs, but I did not come from a very clubbable family. Most of us were refugees, and my elders frowned on drinking, for which Calcutta clubs were infamous. One of my cousins married a man who was reputed to drink, and he was widely considered the black sheep of the family. I had more aunts than Bertie Wooster, and at weddings, they would point him out, nudging each other and whispering about how red his eyes were. He seemed perfectly normal to me, but they remained suspicious. Clubs were widely reputed to be the cause of his downfall.

So that first time, after I got off the minibus and trudged down Jhowtolla Lane, I entered the Dalhousie Institute nervously. I was there to participate in a quiz, or 'squiz', as we called it in Bengali. I can't explain how I got involved in 'squizzing', except that I liked finding out things, and it seemed like a competitive activity with minimal risk of injury. Plus, I was told that there were prizes to be won—books and biscuits and hampers from Hindustan Lever. We were happy with less in those days. But my main reason for going there was Neil O'Brien. We would have bought tickets to take part in a quiz run by him, if they had ever asked us.

Neil was a warm, friendly person. He held it all together. We were a bunch of geeks and freaks, those early quizzers—mixed nuts is the only way to describe us. We came from a variety of backgrounds and incomes and age groups. Ashok Malik, now a senior journalist, used to come directly from school, still in uniform. He was disturbingly well informed. I think I eventually gave up quizzing because I got fed up of constantly losing to a little boy in short pants. Some of the others were pickled old fogies, steeped in Broadway and oil paintings and Shakespeare. Then there were the uncategorizable polymaths, like Partha Basu and Mrs Jayakumar and Devangshu Dutta. It gave me a personal dose of perspective, because until then, I had thought I was smart. They were the brightest group of humans that I have ever hung out with.

If a man is known by the company he keeps, then Neil was a great man indeed. He made us all very welcome. Whether you were in short pants or a Kanjeevaram saree, if you were into quizzing, you were his comrade, and he would always talk to you with the easy familiarity of an equal. Clubs by their very nature are supposed to be exclusive. Whenever I'm in the Delhi Gymkhana or the Bengal Club, for example, I feel like an interloper. I live in constant fear of being exposed as unworthy, and being hauled off by a six-foot tall bearer in a spotless white jacket, held together by a cummerbund and topped off by a turban. Neil never made anyone feel that way, and largely thanks to him, the Dalhousie Institute has to be one of the most egalitarian clubs in the country. The squiz was the thing.

He also changed my perception of alcohol, and its

appropriate usage. I had never actually seen anyone drinking in public before. It was something that you did skulking behind a car at your cousin's wedding, with lookouts posted and breath mints in stock. We were always improbably fragrant. Judging by Hindi movies, I had always assumed that the only activity you could indulge in while drinking was watching cabaret. From observing Neil and the rest of his merry crew, I realized that this was not necessarily the case. It was possible to drink alcohol and do other things also. Beer and quizzing went hand in hand at DI, and no one seemed much worse for wear. As the evening went on, Neil as the quizmaster would sometimes grin a little bit more, and perhaps be a touch more lenient in awarding points, but other than that, he was as sharp as ever.

He was part of a generation who devoted time and energy to quizzing as gentlemanly amateurs. They did it because they loved it. It was a pure art form, like Test cricket, with no newfangled fripperies like buzzer rounds and lifelines and can you identify the cheerleader. Two points for a direct, one for a bonus, and that was it. He was part of a noble breed. Francis Groser, Sadhan Banerjee, R.M. Sinha, Caro Basil—they all slogged away, sometimes with audiences of less than 100 people. But Neil was the prince of them all, and everyone was welcome at his court, greeted by him personally with a pat on the back and a smile. And he always remembered your name.

He was a lovely guy. An incredible number of mixed nuts are going to miss him.

NostalgiCAL

A Mixed Bag

1. Which author has described Calcutta as: 'Thus the midday halt of Charnock—more's the pity! Grew a City'?
2. In 1831, who travelled to the United Kingdom as an ambassador of the Mughal emperor to plead for his pension and allowances?
3. Why was a European policeman paid to stand opposite the Great Eastern Hotel?
4. In 1989, after whom was Elphinstone Picture Palace renamed?
5. On 2 February 1863, who became the first Indian to assume office as a Judge of the Calcutta High Court?
6. Whose statue originally stood on the pedestal, which now has a huge bathtub-like flower pot, in front of Prinsep Ghat?
7. Why was the Grand Hotel shut down in 1933?
8. Who laid the foundation stone of Mahajati Sadan?
9. Which street was originally called Duncan bustee-ka-rasta?
10. Which store gave way to the very first Au Bon Pain in Kolkata?
11. In 1925, who became the first Bengali to be admitted to PG Hospital (later renamed SSKM Hospital) for treatment?
12. In 1947, who established the Institute of Nuclear Physics,

which was later named after him?

13. Before its headquarters was shifted to Calcutta, the National Council of YMCAs of India was formed in which city?

14. Which Bengali enterpreneur owned the steamer *India*?

15. An amount of Rs 1 crore 5 lakh, entirely derived from voluntary subscriptions, was used to build which Calcutta landmark?

16. In the 1780s, who received a grant from Warren Hastings to set up a sugar plantation?

17. In 1907, which scientist came to Calcutta to join the Indian Finance Department as Assistant Accountant General?

18. How is the renowned Bengali writer Balaichand Mukherji better known?

19. On 16 October 1905, Rabindranath Tagore initiated the Raksha Bandhan ceremony and led a procession in Calcutta singing '*Banglar mati Banglar jol*'. What was the occasion?

20. Who edited the first Persian weekly, *Meerut-ul-Akbar*, published from Calcutta in 1822?

21. Who wrote under the pseudonym Tekchand Thakur?

22. What, commissioned in 1943, consumed 26,500 tons of steel and was constructed at an approximate cost of ₹250 lakh?

23. Who devised a statistical method called fractile graphical analysis, which could be used to compare the socio-economic conditions of different groups of people?

24. Who was the first chief minister of West Bengal?

25. What was known as 'company bagaan' (company's garden), till it got a new name in 1857?

PhysiCAL

Sports

1. Which footballer held the post of Sheriff of Kolkata in 2005?

2. Which famous director wrote the lyrics of the KKR official song '*Korbo Lorbo Jeetbo Re*'?

3. In 1958, who became the first Indian to swim across the English Channel?

4. Which team based in Kolkata played in the first three editions of the Pro Kabaddi League?

5. Which Kolkata-born golfer and winner of the Hero Indian Open is nicknamed 'Chipputtsia'?

6. Which stadium was specially constructed to host the World Table Tennis Championships 1975?

7. Poulomi Ghatak and Soumyadeep Roy, both national champions, got married to each other in 2011. In which sport did they represent India?

8. A Royal Bengal tiger along with a Phoenix is the logo of which team?

9. Leander Paes won an Olympic bronze medal in 1996. In which year did his father accomplish the same feat, playing hockey for India?

10. Which brother-sister duo has represented India at the Olympics in Archery (the brother in 2012, the sister in 2004 and 2008)?

11. Name the trophy awarded to the winner of the rugby match between Scotland and England in the Six Nations

Championship.

12. The club house at Eden Gardens is named after which former chief minister of West Bengal?
13. How do we popularly know the famous wrestler Jyotindracharan Guha?
14. In 1991, who became the first Grandmaster in chess from Bengal?
15. How are footballers Appa Rao, P.B. Saleh, K.P. Dhanraj, P. Venkatesh and Ahmed Khan of East Bengal Club collectively known?
16. The first ever FIFA official international friendly match between two foreign nations played on Indian soil was between Argentina and...
17. Who scored the first goal for Mohan Bagan in the match between New York Cosmos and Mohan Bagan in 1977?
18. Who was the first person born in Calcutta to win an Olympic medal?
19. Which Calcuttan is the first Indian golfer to win an event on the US PGA tour?
20. Which Calcuttan captained the Indian team, which won the 1951 Asian Games gold medal in football?
21. Who was the first Calcuttan to captain India in Test cricket?
22. Which Calcuttan was the first Asian to become the

president of the ICC?

23. Which Calcuttan was the first Indian to be ranked junior world number one in squash?

24. On his Ranji Trophy debut, whom did Sourav Ganguly replace in the Bengal team?

25. Who was the first hockey player to compete in four Olympics and also the first to earn 100 international caps for his country?

RadiCAL

Milestones

1. Who, by blocking a part of the Ganges and using other tactics, forced the British to withdraw the taxes they had imposed for fishing in the Ganges?

2. In 1995, who made the first mobile phone call in India to Sukh Ram, the then Communications Minister?

3. Which famous person, born in 1873, established the first Blood Bank in Calcutta?

4. On 7 December 1856, what bold act did Srishchandra Vidyaratna carry out?

5. Which famous wife of a nationalist leader is said to be the first Indian lady to be imprisoned under the British Rule for her involvement in the Indian freedom struggle?

6. Also known as the 'Pavement Doctor', he ran a street clinic for fourteen years providing free medical treatment to the poor in Calcutta. Name him.

7. Which poet was imprisoned on charges of sedition for editing the revolutionary magazine *Dhumketu*?

8. What is Calcutta-based accountant Amitava Banerjee's claim to fame in the medical history of India?

9. For building what, did Goluk Chunder, a blacksmith from Titagarh, win a prize of ₹50 at the Annual Exhibition of the Agri-Horticultural Society, in 1828?

10. Who was conferred the Ramon Magsaysay Award in 1997 for Journalism, Literature, and Creative Communication Arts, 'in recognition of her crusade, through art and

activism, for tribal people to have a just and honorable place in India's national life'?

11. Who edited the journal *Bharati* and formed the 'Sakhi Samiti' or 'Women's Friendly Society' in 1886, one of the first women's organizations in India?

12. Whose ideas of a mass struggle are recorded in the *Historic Eight Documents*?

13. Started in 1868, which famous homeopath and scientist edited the *Calcutta Journal of Medicine*?

14. One morning in 1952, Radhanath Sikdar, a Calcuttan, went to Sir Andrew Waugh's room to announce his great discovery. What was this 'discovery'?

15. Which dancer is credited with the production *Valmiki Pratibha*, involving convicts like Nigel Akkara?

16. In which institution did C V Raman make his historic discovery of the 'Raman Effect'?

17. The first practical steamboat on the Hooghly was launched from Kidderpore dockyard by Kyd and Co. in 1823. What was the name of the gunboat?

18. Who, in the Indian Industrial Exhibition of Calcutta, held in 1906, was awarded a gold medal for his phonographic record?

19. Who was the first person to receive an MA degree in English Literature from Calcutta University?

20. Which poet, born on 25 January 1824, introduced

Amitrakshara, a form of blank verse with varied caesuras, and many other original lyric styles?

21. BBD Bag is named in honour of Benoy Basu, Badal Gupta and ...

22. In 1897, the first-ever Finger Print Bureau in the world was established in Calcutta. Which building housed it?

23. *Debi Chaudhurani* was banned by the British because its patriotic fervour motivated women to come out on the streets. Who was the author of the book?

24. Till the mid 2000s, first time visitors to the city were shocked by graffiti signed by K.C. Paul making an outlandish claim. What was it?

25. What is the name of the son of RCGC greenskeeper, who won the EMAAR-MGF Indian Masters in 2008?

ReCAL

A Mixed Bag

1. Who was the first doctor in India (second in the world) to perform in-vitro fertilization, giving birth to a test tube baby?

2. Who, on losing out to Hensman Anthony in a bard's duel, gave him the name Anthony Kobial?

3. In 2001, who became the first woman to serve as Sheriff of Kolkata?

4. Which first is Dilip Gupta credited with, in the history of Indian cinema?

5. Which scholar reached Calcutta on 25 September 1783 as a Puisne Judge of the Old Supreme Court?

6. Who was the first person to deliver the Convocation Address of Calcutta University in Bengali?

7. Who was the Chairman of the Indian Calendar Reform Committee constituted by the Council of Scientific and Industrial Research in 1952?

8. In 1822, where was the first iron bridge in Calcutta built?

9. Utpal Dutt's 1979 film *Jhor* was based on the life of which famous Calcuttan?

10. Who were the first women graduates of India?

11. Which church houses Job Charnock's tomb?

12. Which organization printed the first stamp in Calcutta in the year 1854?

13. How is Jatindranath Mukherjee popularly known?

14. In 1851, from where was the first message sent to Calcutta through electric telegraph?

15. Which was the first street in the city to be lit by electricity?

16. Which 'first' is Shalom Cohen usually associated with?

17. Who was the first woman to receive the Jnanpith Award?

18. Who called the first strike in Calcutta, in 1827?

19. In 1892, Otis set up India's first elevator in which building in Calcutta?

20. Where would you find the plaque with the words: 'In the small laboratory 70 yards to the south east of this gate Surgeon Major Ronald Ross I.M.S. in 1898 discovered the manner in which malaria is conveyed by mosquitoes.'?

21. Which famous medical practitioner discovered Urea Stibamine, an inorganic compound used in the treatment of Kala-Azar?

22. In 1977, the first statue of a woman put up in Calcutta was that of...

23. What stands at the site where the British constructed the first Fort William?

24. In 1951, which physicist was elected to the Indian Parliament from the North-West Calcutta constituency?

25. Which famous theatre personality wrote his early plays, articles and stories under the assumed names of Botuk, Atanu Lahiri, Sujranjan Chattopadhyay and Kshanesh Prasad Dutta?

The Joy of Living

John Mason

Memories crowd me, as I collect my thoughts on my friend and mentor Neil O'Brien. My first impressions of Neil were as a publisher. It was 1976, and Neil had just accepted my manuscript for a textbook. Consequently, I was a regular visitor to Oxford University Press, Calcutta, where Neil was the regional manager. As I hung around the office, I observed the reverence the staff had for Mr O'Brien.

'He was a colossus in publishing,' says my friend Aloke Roychowdhury, who edited the textbook back then. 'He knew the market better than anybody. It was uncanny, the way he would evaluate a typescript. If he chose to publish, the book did well.'

Neil had a phenomenal memory. Aloke remembers accompanying him on a flight from Calcutta to Delhi. Neil was poring over a heavy tome of facts on the English soccer league. He passed the book over to Aloke after some time. 'Ask me any question,' he challenged. 'I'll answer.' And Neil did!

But there was something more than his rattling memory. Neil O'Brien had good taste, testimony of which was the wide range of books he published. He had a donnish humour and a taste for pithy aphorisms. I still remember this one: 'Two people you can't hide your secrets from are your tailor and your publisher!'

He was the father of quizzing. I think he remained bemused over this unprovoked paternity. 'It started innocently enough,' he once explained. 'Some of us would gather at the club and there would be a few rounds of questions and drinks, that's all.'

I was witness to the phenomenon when dozens of teams participated and a thousand-strong audience thronged the finals at Dalhousie Institute in Calcutta. The attraction of a Neil O'Brien quiz was the novelty of his questions and his meticulous reliability.

In fact, I was a beneficiary of the craze. Doordarshan invited me to do the occasional children's quiz on television, which I enjoyed possibly more than the children. In 1982, I was in a boat on Dal Lake with my family when another boat accosted us. 'Are you from Calcutta?' said a man in the party .

'Yes!' I replied, surprised.

'Do you do quiz?'

'Oh, he's recognized me,' I whispered to my family. 'Yes, I do,' I said aloud.

'Are you Neil O'Brien?' was the next question.

It was inevitable that Neil would fulfil a challenging social and political role and, being a people's person, he not only filled that space but also enhanced its value. In 1978, Neil was MLA when the service staff of St James' School, where I was principal, went on strike. It was a trying time for the school as tempers were running high. Neil came forward to help. Here was a different man to the one I knew. Detached when others were involved, cool when others were overheated, and quiet amidst the theatrical din. Neil guided us to a settlement that was fair for the school and the staff. By these and other actions, Neil O'Brien won the respect of the community and the government.

As an Anglo-Indian, Neil had a profound yet affectionate understanding of the culture of the community. Within the community, he laughed at its foibles but he was a doughty opponent of those who, in his judgement, made light of the character of the community in print or on film.

Despite the nature of his responsibilities, Neil lived simply and with his devoted wife Joyce who supported his work with fervour and raised a remarkable family. He epitomized the community that celebrates the joy of living.

SabbatiCAL

Leisure

1. Which club, established in 1907, started admitting women members in 2007?

2. Which club was founded by a Scottish banker, William Dixon Cruickshank, on the land owned by Tipu Sultan's descendants?

3. Which club, established in 1920 and located on Woodburn Park Road, has been a venue to Davis Club matches?

4. What, adjacent to Alipore Zoo, was founded by William Carey in 1820?

5. After whom was the Surendranath Park, situated opposite Raj Bhavan, originally named?

6. Which hotel was referred to as 'the best hotel East of the Suez' by Mark Twain?

7. In which hotel would you find a pub named Someplace Else?

8. Where would you find the bar called Light Horse Bar, housing the trophies won by the Calcutta Light Horse Regiment?

9. Which is said to be the oldest golf club in India and second oldest in the world?

10. In which year was the Nicco Park opened to the public?

11. In 1942, it was set up as the 'Swiss Club'. Later, its present name was selected from amongst other suggested names like Eidelwiss Club, After Eight Club and Phoenix Club .

How do we know it today?

12. Lord Minto, the Viceroy of India, wanted to invite Rajen Mookerjee to dine at the Bengal Club. He was not allowed to do so because the club allowed only whites. As a result of this incident, a club was founded with a membership policy not dictated by race. Name the club.

13. Sabuj Sathi, Graffiti Walls and Rabi Aranya are some of the attractions of which landmark?

14. Who was the President of the Bengal Club from 1827–37?

15. In 2007, the Citizen's Park, near Victoria Memorial, was renamed Mohor Kunja in honour of...

16. In 1908, Maharaja Dhiraja Sri Bijoy Chand Mahtab of ______ became the first Indian to receive full membership of the Calcutta Turf Club. Fill in the blank.

17. In which heritage plaza would you find a traditional crafts village named Shilpgram, an urban zone named Sambhar, and a food park called Santushti?

18. Who was the first president of The Calcutta South India Club, founded in 1926?

19. Inside which landmark, inaugurated on 1 July 1997, would you come across the Dynamotion Hall, Space Theatre, and Evolution Park?

20. In which theme park in Kolkata would you come across the Niagra Fall, the Black Hole, and the Surf Racer?

21. The foundation stone of which club was laid on 4 March

1865 by the Lieutenant Governor of Bengal, the Hon'ble Cecil Beadon?

22. The open air theatre, Nazrul Mancha, is located near which artificial lake in Kolkata?

23. In Kolkata, what was opened to the public on 1 May 1876?

24. In which shopping mall would you find Amoeba, a gaming and entertainment zone?

25. The Indian Life Saving Society is popularly known as…

SymboliCAL

Customs and Traditions

1. Which organization became one of the first to celebrate Sarbojonin Durga Puja in Calcutta, after adopting an idea by Atindra Nath Bose?

2. What is the significance of Sandhi Puja, performed during Durga Puja?

3. On which day is the auspicious task of painting Goddess Durga's eyes, known as 'chokkhudaan', traditionally performed?

4. Which was the first talkie film in Bengali (Hint: named after a Bengali ritual)?

5. During Durga Puja, who begins life as 'nabapatrika'?

6. How did the phrase 'daaker saaj' marking the reputation of the Daw family of North Calcutta, originate?

7. Tradition calls for the five images (Durga, Lakshmi, Saraswati, Kartik and Ganesh) to be sculpted on one common base (ek chaala). However, today these images also stand separately. How did the latter tradition start?

8. What is the ceremony of 'hatey khori'?

9. According to superstition, which fruit should not be eaten till Saraswati Puja?

10. According to the panjika by Benimadhab Seal, a mole under an eye signifies…

11. The major football clubs in Calcutta, along with other small sports clubs, perform which special ritual on Poila Boishakh?

12. What does the tradition of opening a 'halkhata' signify?

13. While laying the foundation stone of Bethune school, Mr Bethune got an Ashoka tree planted. What did the Ashoka tree signify?

14. Traditionally, which bird was ceremoniously released during idol immersion on Dashami to symbolize Devi Durga's departure?

15. When gods were giving Devi Durga her weapons, which weapon did Viswakarma give her?

16. Outside which temple would you find the Panchavati tree, a site where Sri Ramakrishna performed the Panchamundi (5 skulls) Ashana?

17. The winners of the first Asian Paints Sharad Samman in 1995 were Adi Ballygunge, Jodhpur Park and...

18. Who is the Hindu goddess of smallpox?

19. In an annaprashan in a Bengali family, a child is offered a few objects on a plate, including pen, money and soil. The choice of the object is said to reflect his/her inclination. What would the child be inclined towards if he/she chooses a pen?

20. According to the panjika by Benimadhab Seal, what will one get if a lizard falls on the palm?

21. What is referred to as 'bouni' by traders?

22. Where would you find Highwayshwari or highway goddess, existing in the form of a rock?

23. What tradition was introduced by Laksmikanta Mazumdar, who started the Aatchala Barisha Puja, one of the oldest Durga Pujas in Calcutta?

24. According to the panjika by Benimadhab Seal, if you dream of travelling by air, what does it signify?

25. The potters of Kumortuli perform the Kathamo Puja before starting work on the idols for the Durga Puja. On which famous festival is it traditionally held?

TactiCAL

Administration

1. Which rank of Calcutta Police was meant for British officers transferred to Indian police forces from the East India Company's European regiments, to maintain discipline and to instruct them in foot and rifle drill and weapons-handling?

2. Who was the first Indian Commissioner of Police in Calcutta?

3. Towards the middle of the nineteenth century, which specialized professionals did William Coats Blacquiere, a city magistrate, introduce to systematize policing in Calcutta?

4. In the early eighteenth century, who were known as the 'black zamindars' in the administrative system?

5. What is the apolitical titular position of authority that only Calcutta and Mumbai still maintain?

6. Who abolished the post of Naib-Diwans in Bengal and removed the treasury to Calcutta when he became governor in 1772?

7. For what commendable contribution was Sukumar Sen celebrated as a hero in Ramachandra Guha's book *India After Gandhi*?

8. From where did Dr B.C. Roy source the funds for the film *Pather Panchali*?

9. Which grand edifice is the headquarters of the Eastern Command of the Indian Army?

10. Who first formalised and set up the Detective Department in November 1868, with A. Younan as the superintendent and R. Lamb as the first-class inspector?

11. Who fought his famous duel with Philip Francis on the grounds of Belvedere Estate?

12. The place where once stood the residence of John Palmer, a merchant, is now the headquarters of…

13. On 1 November 1858, a group of Englishmen from Calcutta was organized into a Pipe-Band to play at the Governor's House. What was the occasion?

14. Job Charnock purchased the villages of Kalikata, Sutanuti and Govindpur from which famous family?

15. In the Raj Bhavan, in which room are incoming governors administered the Oath of Office?

16. Who served as the Mayor of Kolkata from 22 August 1930 to 14 April 1931?

17. Sir Fredrick Halliday created which branch of the Calcutta Police in June 1909?

18. Which Indian president was a legal practitioner in Calcutta in 1911, apprenticed to Khan Bahadur Shamsul Huda?

19. What is inscribed on the top in old Bengali script on the current emblem of the Kolkata Municipal Corporation?

20. What was first introduced in 1840 by the Calcutta Police, with only two sowars under a dafadar (head officer) to

carry messages and inform the harbour master whenever any ship was sighted?

21. Who was the first Chief Justice of the High Court of Judicature at Fort William when it formally opened on 1 July 1862?

22. Who was the self-proclaimed governor of Bengal when the Black Hole tragedy took place?

23. Who captured Calcutta on 2 January 1757, and forced Siraj-ud-Daula to restore British East India Company's privileges, pay compensation, and allow the British to fortify Calcutta?

24. After Independence, who is the first woman to have occupied the Raj Bhavan as the governor of West Bengal?

25. Which practice, introduced in the Bengal Legislative Council on 31 January 1934, continues to this day though there is no provision of the same in the Constitution of India?

TheatriCAL

The Stage

1. The famous playwright Girish Chandra Ghosh was a devotee of which saint?
2. Which famous theatre was destroyed a fire that broke out in Kolkata in November 1843?
3. Iswarchandra Vidyasagar's *Bhrantibilas* was based on which play by William Shakespeare?
4. From which play has Tapan Sinha's *Bancharam er bagan* been adapted?
5. Which actor established Srirangam, now known as Bishwarupa theatre?
6. Which play, set against the backdrop of the Bengal famine, revolves around the life of Pradhan Samaddar?
7. Who played the role of Alik babu in the Bengali farce of the same name by Jyotindranath Tagore?
8. Who directed *Komal Gandhar,* a film revolving around the rivalry between two radical theatre groups?
9. *Ruddhasangeet*, a play by Bratya Basu, chronicles the life of which personality?
10. Tapas Sen earned the nickname Tapas 'light' Sen for depicting a catastrophic flooding of coal mines through light in which play?
11. Which theatre group started the National Theatre Festival in 1984 under the leadership of Rudra Prasad Sengupta?
12. Who formed the group Shatabdi, whose first production was *Evam Indrajit*?

13. Which former Lok Sabha MP and Union minister played the role of Ramakrishna in the play *Noti Binodini*?

14. Which actress, whose stage-life lasted from the age of 12 to 23, recounts her life in her autobiography titled *Amar Katha*?

15. Who organized the dramatic troupe *Bohurupee* and went on to win the Ramon Magsaysay Award in 1976?

16. In 1872, who founded the National Theatre, the first Bengali professional company?

17. In 1795, who became the first person to present a Bengali play in the city, when he staged a Bengali translation of an English comedy called *The Disguise*?

18. Which actor, born in 1929, founded Calcutta Little Theatre Group in 1947?

19. Which actor was known as Dani Babu?

20. In 1858, who wrote *Sharmistha*, popularly referred to as the first original play in Bengali?

21. In 2015, which theatre personality was the host of the reality show *Happy Parents Day*?

22. She received the Sangeet Natak Akademi Award in 1998. She set up a theatre group named Rangakarmee in 1976. Name her.

23. Which theatre personality played the role of Durga in Ritwik Ghatak's *Jukti Takko Aar Gappo*?

24. Which theatre, built in 1883, was initially situated on Beadon Street?

25. Which play by Rabindranatha Tagore was initially titled *Yakshapuri*?

TheologiCAL

Religion

1. After the 1834 Calcutta earthquake, the tower of which cathedral was rebuilt along the lines of the Bell Harry Tower in Canterbury Cathedral?

2. Which church is sometimes referred to as the 'pathure girja'?

3. In which temple of a Hindu deity is chopsuey and noodles offered as bhog in Calcutta?

4. The foundation stone of which church was laid by Archibald Seton on 30 November 1815?

5. Which member of royalty built the Tipu Sultan Mosque in Esplanade and Shaheed Tipu Sultan Shahi Mosque in Tollygunge?

6. By what name is St James' Church in Calcutta popularly known?

7. 'By work alone, men may get to where Buddha got largely by meditation or Christ by prayer. Buddha was a working Jnani, Christ was a Bhakta, but the same goal was reached by both of them.' Who said these words?

8. According to legend, which body part of Sati fell on the site of the Kalighat Temple?

9. To whom is the main temple of the Parshwanath Jain Temple, located on Bodridas Lane, dedicated?

10. In 2008, who became the first brand ambassador of a Durga Puja organized by the Badamtala Ashar Sangha?

11. The decision to build what near the site then known as

the 'Fives Court' was taken in 1839?

12. On which street is the Late Ervad Dhunjeebhoy Byramjee Mehta's Zoroastrian Anjuman Atash Adaran, established in 1912, located?

13. The founder of Scottish Church College was also the first missionary to India from the Church of Scotland. Name him.

14. A large section of which community worships at the Sea Ip Temple?

15. Which temple, located in Southern Avenue, was founded by Haripada Chakrabarty?

16. These are the opening lines of a prayer: 'Dearest Lord, may I see you today and everyday in the person of your sick, and while nursing them minister unto you.' Who wrote this prayer?

17. The Nakhoda Mosque in Calcutta is modelled after which Mughal Emperor's tomb?

18. Which temple, dedicated to Siddheshwari Mata, was founded by Sankar Ghosh?

19. Who are the members of the Sathi Brahman Sangathan?

20. Who laid the foundation stone of St John's Church on 8 April 1787?

21. Who established the only Japanese Buddhist temple in Calcutta, located on the southern fringe of Rabindra Sarobar?

22. Name the first Anglican Bishop of Calcutta.

23. Who visited Prome in 1853 and shipped the Burmese Pagoda to Calcutta, which arrived on 29 September 1854, and was stored in Fort William before a suitable site could be found for it?

24. In which church would you find Johann Zoffany's oil painting *Last Supper*?

25. Vishwa Mangal Trust, 29 Ashutosh Choudhury Avenue, Kolkata-19 is the address of which temple?

VehiCAL

Transport

1. Between which two stations was the first Metro service opened for public in 1984?

2. In 1905, it was established by a French Armenian diamond merchant Micheal Sevadjian at Calcutta. In 1925 Sir Onkarmal Jatia became its first Indian Director. Name the company.

3. In 1834, who launched Carr, Tagore & Co. in partnership with William Carr?

4. Who laid the foundation stone of the Metro Rail on 29 December 1972?

5. What is the colour of the band on the 'No Refusal' taxis introduced in 2013?

6. Which heritage tramcar, introduced by Calcutta Tramways Company, is named after a character created by Jibananda Das?

7. In Kolkata, you would dial 101 for which emergency service?

8. What is the name of the 2003 film in which Avinash (Anil Kapoor) meets Rima (Rani Mukherjee) a novelist in Calcutta?

9. In 1933, what did Sripati Charan Kundu introduce to India when he reserved an entire train and undertook a 56-day all-India tour?

10. In 2009, who was the Garia Bazar metro station named after?

11. On 15 August 1854, the first train of East Indian Railway commenced its inaugural commercial run from Howrah to...
12. In which film does Shambhu Mahato ply a hand-pulled rickshaw in Calcutta to pay off his debt?
13. Bepin Behari Das was the first Indian to build a motor car in its entirety. What was this first Indian motor car named?
14. Which kind of horse-drawn vehicle was named after the occupation of its passengers, the clerks?
15. Which poet, born on 17 February 1899, died in a tram accident in 1954?
16. The first double-decker bus in Calcutta plied between ______ and Kalighat. Fill in the blank.
17. In January 1941, who escaped from his house in a Wanderer, bearing the number BLA-7169?
18. By what name are the horse-drawn carriages plying around Victoria Memorial popularly known?
19. Which train, the country's first point-to-point non-stop train, was flagged off in September 2009 from Sealdah?
20. From which airport did the maiden flight of the West Bengal government's helicopter service take off, in 2013?
21. The country's first air-conditioned double-decker train, flagged off in 2011, ran between Howrah and _____. Fill in the blank.

22. A tram, built in 1938, has been converted into a mobile museum to exhibit tram memorabilia associated with the history of trams. Name it.

23. The people of which community introduced the rickshaw in Calcutta in the late nineteenth century?

24. In 2009, Kudghat metro station was named after which freedom fighter?

25. On 24 February 1873, the first tram in Kolkata ran between ______ and Armenian Ghat Street. Fill in the blank.

VertiCAL

Buildings

1. Which landmark stands at 1, Queens Way, Kolkata 700071?

2. Which building, built between 1799 and 1803, is modelled on Kedleston Hall in Derbyshire, the ancestral house of Lord Curzon?

3. What name did Lord Minto give to the building the 'Palace to the Arts', completed by Rajendra Mallik in around 1840?

4. Who was the owner of the land on which Stephen Court now stands?

5. Which Calcutta-based company built the Victoria Memorial?

6. In 1777, Thomas Lyon was asked to construct a building in Calcutta. At the time of its completion in 1780, it is said to have been the first three-storey construction in Calcutta. Name it.

7. Adjoining which metro station is the age-old building Dhurjati Dham (one of the suites of rooms and halls on the first floor was used by Satyajit Ray for shooting Jalsaghar) located?

8. The west front of which building on Strand Road (that is also the model for BNR House) has been modelled on the Tower of Winds in Athens?

9. In which old heritage building is the Maritime Archives and Heritage Centre housed?

10. Which monument on Strand Road is known to many as 'the pepper pot'?

11. Which building was designed by Mr Walter Granville on the model of the 'Stadt-Haus' or Cloth Hall, at Ypres, in Belgium?

12. Where did the Bengal Legislative Council sit from 1 February 1921 to 8 February 1931?

13. How was the money for the construction of Elliot Road, Strand Road, Wellington Street, Cornowalish Street, Rawdan Street, the Town Hall and the Belliaghata Canal obtained?

14. Who inaugurated Nandan in September 1985 and also named the institution?

15. The Indian Museum, founded in 1814, was initially housed at 1, Park Street, which is the present address of...

16. With which famous person would you associate the house at 3, Gour Mohan Mukherjee Street?

17. In 2013, the Chief Secretariat of the Government of West Bengal shifted to a new building sharing its name with a play by Bijon Bhattacharya. Name the play.

18. The East Gate of which historical monument was formerly called the Plassey Gate?

19. By which famous architect was the City Centre in Salt Lake designed?

20. Which was the first 20-floor plus building in Kolkata

when it was constructed in 1976?

21. Which is the first mall in Calcutta with multi-level car park?

22. The Shahid Minar is a rare combination of three architectural styles. The column is Syrian, the dome with its metal cupola is Turkish, while the base is...

23. What was the old name of Gandhi Bhavan at Beliaghata?

24. Which leader's ancestral house is located at 38/2, Lala Lajpat Rai Sarani, Kolkata-700 020?

25. When it was built, what was the 'football' on top of the New Secretariat building used for?

VoCAL

Famous Quotes

1. 'The people of Kolkata, these well educated and aware people of Kolkata, have great manners and awareness of anything that is everything...such a delight to be in their midst.' Whose words are these?

2. Who said: 'What is the use of Bengal without Calcutta'?

3. Who said, 'I come to Calcutta as Vasco da Gama. It's a polemic. I'm explaining my broken love for Calcutta. You only come back if you love something'?

4. Which actress said, 'I've shot three films (*Parineeta*, *No One Killed Jessica* and *Kahaani*) ... and yes, I think I was a Bengali in my last birth'?

5. Who called Calcutta 'In short, I will pronounce Calcutta to be one of the most wicked places in the Universe'?

6. Who, in his book *Calcutta: Two Years in the City,* wrote, 'Bombay is about money; Delhi about power; Calcutta is about parents'?

7. Who said: 'Calcutta is a monstrous, teeming, bewildering city'?

8. Who called Calcutta a 'humbug of palaces'?

9. In 2015, which footballer said, 'Thank you for the beautiful reception...I love Kolkata...I am here because I love the people here'.

10. Who, in 2011, said, 'As you honour me today by conferring on me the Honoris Causa, I express my profound sense of gratitude to the University of Calcutta.'

11. After the victory of Kolkata Knight Riders in the 2012 IPL, who said 'I think Delhiites know how to party, but Kolkata has people who know how to celebrate. I think that's the main difference'?

12. 'So in the streets of Calcutta I sometimes imagine myself a foreigner, and only then do I discover how much is to be seen, which is lost so long as its full value in attention is not paid. It is the hunger to really see which drives people to travel to strange places.' Whose words are these?

13. '*Dil ka bazaar hai, thoda bizzare hai, Kolkata khwaishon armaano ka achaar hai.*' These are words from a song from which film?

14. Who said, 'In a global economy where the best jobs follow talent—whether in Kolkata or Cleveland—we need to do everything we can to encourage that same kind of passion, make it easier for more young people to blaze a new trail'?

15. Whose first impression of the city was: 'I shall always be glad to have seen it—for the same reason Papa gave for being glad to have seen Lisbon—namely, that it will be unnecessary for me ever to see it again'?

16. Which author found the weather of Calcutta 'enough to make the brass doorknob mushy'?

17. Who observed, 'Calcutta without a bandh is like Shakespeare's *Hamlet* without the Prince of Denmark'?

18. Who said, 'You want your cities clean and green; stick to

Delhi. You want your cities, rich and impersonal, go to Bombay. You want them high-tech and full of draught beer, Bangalore's your place. But if you want a city with a soul, come to Calcutta'?

19. Who said, 'Find, if you can, a more uninviting spot than Calcutta...The place is so bad by nature that human efforts could do little to make it worse'?

20. In 1963, which famous author called Calcutta 'an abomination'?

21. Who predicted: 'The road to revolution lies through Peking, Shanghai and Calcutta'?

22. Who paid the city this tribute: 'I bow my head to Calcutta and Calcuttans in gratitude for giving me more than what I expected—a debt which I can never repay'?

23. 'One of the regrets of my career is that I never scored heavily in Calcutta and thus savour the applause of over 90,000 spectators at Eden Gardens, one of cricket's great venues.' Who had this regret?

24. 'The players might come from all over the world but they are all so emotional about Kolkata. Somehow each one of them believes that Kolkata is their home. The people of Kolkata have supported us through our disgustingly bad phase and then the champion phases. Aami KKR!' These are the words of which famous personality?

25. Who sang the song '*Ami Miss Calcutta 1976*' from the film *Basanta Bilap*?

ANSWERS

AcademiCAL (Education)

1. Iswarchandra Vidyasagar. He served as the principal from 1851 to 1858.
2. St Xavier's College
3. Jagadish Chandra Bose. Later he was given his full salary which he used for paying off his father's debt.
4. South Point High School. South Point had the distinction of winning a place in the Guinness Book of World Records (1984–1992) as the then world's largest school.
5. Dwarkanath Tagore
6. Scottish Church College
7. Henry Louis Vivian Derozio
8. Satyajit Ray
9. St Thomas' School, Kidderpore
10. Suniti Kumar Chattopadhyay. After retirement he was made Professor Emeritus and, in 1963, National Professor.
11. Sakhawat Memorial Government Girls' High School

12. Bankim Chandra Chattopadhyay. Graduated in 1858. He started his literary career with the English novel *Rajmohan's Wife*.

13. Modern High School for Girls

14. Rashi Vigyan or Rashi Vidya. Rabindranath Tagore also wrote a poem for the inaugural issue of the Journal of Indian Statistical Institute.

15. Kadambini Ganguly

16. Bethune College. It started as the Hindu Female School in 1849 and blossomed into the Bethune School.

17. Basanti Devi

18. Loreto House

19. Maulana Abul Kalam Azad

20. La Martiniere Schools

21. St Mary's School

22. Bidhan Chandra Roy

23. Armenian College and Philanthropic Academy

24. Rabindranath Tagore

25. Gooroodass Banerjee

AesthetiCAL (The Arts)

1. Victoria Memorial

2. Lalmohan Ganguly aka Jatayu

3. Protul Chandra Sorcar (P.C. Sorcar, Sr)
4. *Chowringhee* by Shankar
5. Rabindranath Tagore
6. Satyajit Ray
7. Mitin Mashi
8. Samaresh Basu
9. Byomkesh Bakshi
10. Abanindranath Tagore
11. Anand Nagar
12. Michael Madhusudan Dutta
13. Manik Bandopadhyay
14. Jamini Roy
15. Pakhir neer (Bird's nest)
16. Bankim Chandra Chattopadhyay
17. Rajnikanta Sen
18. Michael Atherton
19. *The Lowland*
20. Desmond Doig
21. Yaksha and Yakshini
22. Sir Ronald Ross

23. Upendrakishore Ray
24. Katum Kutum
25. Jnanadanandini Devi

CinematiCAL (Films)

1. *Kanchenjunga*
2. Srijit Mukherji
3. Manik Bandopadhyay, Prabodh Sanyal and Samaresh Basu
4. St Xavier's College. It is the social communication centre sponsored by the Kolkata Province of the Society of Jesus founded with the support of Satyajit Ray.
5. Apu Nahasapeemapetilon. After Apu from the Apu trilogy directed by Satyajit Ray.
6. *Mukti*
7. Uttam Kumar
8. Tollywood
9. Rituparno Ghosh
10. *Jukti Takko ar Gappo*
11. Gautam Ghose
12. Rafeeq Ellias
13. *36 Chowringhee Lane*

14. Rabindranath Tagore himself. Tagore played the role of Upala. Nitin Bose cinematographed the film and Subodh Mitra edited it. It was released at Chitra Talkies on 14 March 1932.
15. Amitabh Bachchan
16. Uttam Kumar
17. Rickshaw puller
18. Dev or Deepak Adhikari
19. Parambrata Chatterjee
20. *Tahader Kotha*
21. *15 Park Avenue*
22. Victor Bannerjee
23. Soumitra Chatterjee
24. Amitabh Bachchan
25. Jean Renoir

ComiCAL (The Lighter Side)

1. *Haashte*
2. *Hirak Rajar Deshe*
3. *Lukochuri*
4. *Bhooter Bhobishyot*
5. Moustache

6. Rabi Ghosh

7. Kyabla

8. Roadside salons operated by barbers who make their customers sit on a brick

9. Krishnachandra

10. Narayan Debnath

11. Keshab Sen, the Bramho leader; Wil-Sen or 'Wilson's Hotel', where Hindus would guzzle 'forbidden food'; and the 'Isti-sen' or station, as the niceties of caste could not be observed on railway journeys.

12. Sanjib Chattopadhyay

13. *Gouri*

14. Manohar Aich

15. Columbus

16. Bati. Taking 'Ba' from 'bangal' (people from East Bengal) and 'ti' from 'ghoti' (people from West Bengal)

17. Edward Lear

18. Hrishikesh Mukherjee

19. *Sharey Chuattar*

20. Harshabardhan and Gobardhan

21. *Ogo Bodhu Shundori*

22. Kaliprasanna Singha

23. Corruption of Duke, a brand of cricket balls
24. Phoo-phoo band
25. Mir

EconomiCAL (Business)

1. Duckback
2. Dabur
3. Birla Jute Manufacturing Company Ltd
4. Sir Rajendranath Mookerjee
5. ITC
6. Orient Electric
7. The Calcutta Stock Exchange
8. Subhas Chandra Bose
9. Mother Teresa
10. Quest Mall
11. Bijoli Grill
12. Elephant
13. Dwarkanath Tagore
14. R.P. Goenka
15. Kolkata Port Trust
16. Panjika or Bengali Almanac

17. Sanjiv Goenka
18. Margo soap
19. Acharya Prafulla Chandra Ray
20. G.D. Birla
21. *The Statesman*
22. India Government Mint, Kolkata
23. The Ruia Group led by Mr Pawan Kumar Ruia
24. Amitabh Bachchan
25. Oriental Life Insurance Company

GastronomiCAL (Food)

1. Potato
2. Dahi (curd)
3. Daab Sherbat
4. Ledikeni
5. Nahoum Israel Mordecai, who set up Nahoum's
6. *'Coffee Houser shei addata...'*
7. Yauatcha
8. Payodhi
9. Aabaar Khabo
10. A corruption of the word 'braised'

11. Kathi Roll at Nizam's
12. Eau Chew
13. Nolen gurer Sandesh
14. Lentil puff
15. The menu card called 'Kromoni'
16. Kosha mangsho
17. Allen Kitchen
18. Manna Dey
19. Au Bon Pain
20. Dhoper Chop
21. Taj Bengal
22. Chana-jor-Garam
23. Chelo Kebab
24. Akshay Tritiya
25. Flury's

GeographiCAL (Roads)

1. Park Street
2. Manna De
3. Barrackpore Trunk
4. William Shakespeare

5. Boi Para in College Street
6. Gurusaday Dutta
7. The Netaji Indoor Stadium
8. Deshapriya Park. It was organized by the INA Relief Committee and addressed by Sarat Bose, Nehru and Patel. Lakhs of people attended.
9. Ezra Street
10. Babu Ghat Bus Stand. The military band performed from here.
11. The Dominique Lapierre City of Joy Village
12. 'September on Jessore Road'
13. Tipu Sultan
14. Iswarchandra Vidyasagar
15. Wajid Ali Shah
16. Ma
17. Sri Chaitanya
18. Ho Chin Minh
19. Picasso
20. Chief Justice of the Supreme Court
21. James Outram's equestrian statue
22. Suchitra Mitra

23. Shyambazar five-point crossing
24. Vidyapati Setu
25. Golf Green

HistoriCAL (The Past)

1. The National Library
2. Tagore/Thakur
3. *Vande Mataram*
4. Eden Gardens
5. Town Hall
6. Telephone Exchange in Calcutta. The exchange at Calcutta was named 'Central Exchange'.
7. Jagdish Chandra Bose
8. Chittaranjan Das
9. Subhas Chandra Bose
10. Willian Hedges
11. Zamindar
12. Siraj-ud-Daulah named it after his grandfather Alivardi Khan after defeating the British in 1756.
13. Swami Vivekananda. The first reason was to gain the acceptance of the local community for the new way of life that he was leading. He also wanted to institutionalize

respect for divinity of motherhood and sanctity of womanhood.

14. *Hickey's Bengal Gazette*

15. The Indian Association Building

16. Green

17. Shaheed Minar. Previously called Ochterlony Monument, it was rechristened as the 'Shaheed Minar' in memory of the Indian freedom fighters, in 1969.

18. Maidan

19. *Tottvobodhini Patrika*

20. Satyendranath Tagore

21. Richard Wellesley

22. Womesh Chandra Bonnerjee

23. There was a problem with his exact age.

24. Murshidabad

25. Raja Ram Mohan Roy

LexiCAL (Origins)

1. It was a colony of artisans who fashioned the clay from the river into pots, mostly to be sold at Sutanuti Bazar. These artisans were known as Kumor or Kumbhakar, from which the place got its name.

2. Job Charnock used to conduct his business sitting

underneath a banyan tree in Sealdah. Often Britishers use to gather at this place for informal chit-chat.

3. The temple of Chitreshwari might have given the locality its name or it might have come from the name of the notorious bandit of that area, 'Chitey Dakat'.

4. 'Majum' meant 'sum' in Arabic. The basic job of the Majumders was to keep account of the government collections.

5. There is the record of a creek, which originally ran from Chandpal Ghat to Baliaghata (present-day Beleghata), which gives the road its name. The earlier name of Creek Row was Dhinga Bhanga, a ship having broken there during the cyclone of 1737.

6. Baroari Puja means a puja arranged and organized entirely by the local community. It is said to have been first organized in Guptipara, a place about 100 km away from Kolkata. The word 'Baroari' came from Baro (twelve in Bengali) + yaar (friends).

7. Designed in 1841, it was named after the Eden sisters of Lord Auckland, then the British Governor General of India.

8. It is named after a Frenchman, or as some say, a Venetian, named Edward Tiretta, who was the superintendant of streets and buildings. The market was valued at two lakhs and when Tirreta became bankrupt, his creditors gave it away at that sum as a prize.

9. It was built during the days of the East India Company to provide shelter to the junior writers or clerks of the Company.

10. It was named after Colonel Henry Watson, who set up the first dockyards in Bengal.

11. People belonging to the Mukhoti village of the Bankura district had this surname.

12. Most probably the name came from the 'tangra' fish, the popular catch before the area was reclaimed.

13. It was the residential quarters of the paiks or native watchmen who acted as policemen and were also employed by wealthy Indians as guards.

14. According to a version, it derived its name from the Hintal, a species of date palm that grew on tidal land.

15. It was founded by Shobharam Basak but named after the diety Shyam Ray or Govinda.

16. It was named after the Armenian merchant Peter Sukeas who allowed the public to take water from his tank.

17. Intially it was named after 'Buro' or Shiva. Later, the merchants changed it to Barabazar, meaning 'big market'.

18. It was the home of the Company's 'Kaluas' or oil-pressers who used to supple mustard and other kinds of oil.

19. A fast courier on foot

20. Popularly believed that it is named after Jungal Gir

Chowringhee, a pious worshipper of Shiva, whose hermitage was located inside a dense forest that is now Chowringhee. He was the founder of a sect who were also known by his name.

21. The surname belonged to lac-traders.

22. It got its name from 'kankurs', a species of melon, which grew in plenty in that area.

23. Comes from the word 'buniad' meaning 'base'. Means something which is old, established and venerated.

24. The area lay outside the Maratha ditch. The name may have come from 'ulta dingi' meaning an upturned boat. It may refer to an accident or boats being upturned for repair.

25. A male cook, who often also assumes the role of house steward.

LoCAL (A Mixed Bag)

1. Kolkata Book Fair

2. Kolkata Police

3. Films. It is awarded at the Kolkata International Film Festival (KIFF).

4. La Martiniere to Pratt Memorial School

5. Usha Uthup

6. Tenida

7. W.M. Thackeray
8. *Battleship Potemkin*
9. Uttam Kumar
10. www.kumartuli.com
11. *Tattvabodhini Patrika*
12. Spices
13. C.R. Das
14. Tollygunge. The name Russapugla comes from a unique tree which gave shade to Pugla Pir who meditated and died in the area.
15. Watches or clocks
16. Chrysanthemum
17. The Lalit Great Eastern Hotel
18. Satyajit Ray
19. Missie Baba
20. Lord Clive. It was gifted to the zoo in 1875 and died in 2006. Adwaita means 'the one and only' in Sanskrit.
21. Bhabanicharan Bandyopadhyay
22. Kakababu
23. Stephen Owen Moses
24. Esplanade

25. Milkmen

MusiCAL (Music)

1. Trinca's
2. Salil Chowdhury
3. Anupam Roy
4. Calcutta Youth Choir
5. Nikhil Banerjee
6. The Calcutta School of Music
7. Debasish Bhattacharya
8. Bhoomi
9. Moheener Ghoraguli
10. Kabir Suman
11. Kazi Nazrul Islam
12. Gauhar Jaan
13. Tappa
14. Chandrabindu
15. Talat Mahmood
16. Manna Dey
17. Rupam Islam
18. Jadunath Bhattacharya

19. Usha Uthup
20. Anjan Dutt
21. Begum Akhtar
22. *Pride & Glory: The Story of Calcutta*
23. Pankaj Kumar Mullick. Eventually that song was approved by Tagore himself.
24. Nachiketa
25. Hemanta Kumar Mukhopadhyay

NautiCAL (Water bodies)

1. Princep Ghat after James Princep
2. From the local name for marshy land-haor
3. Kidderpore
4. Bula Chowdhury
5. The Indian Seamen who took part in the First World War
6. Bidhan Chandra Roy
7. At Fort William the deep borehole struck fresh water at a depth of 51.8 metres.
8. Tolly Nullah
9. Diamond Harbour
10. Rani Rashmoni. Babu Raj Chandra Das was Rani Rashmoni's husband.

11. Suriname
12. Dhakuria Lake or Rabindra Sarobar
13. Vidyasagar Setu (Also known as the Second Hooghly Bridge)
14. Chhotulal Ghat
15. Nivedita Setu
16. Babu Ghat
17. Maratha Ditch
18. Komagata Maru
19. Maharaja Durga Charan Laha
20. Netaji Subhas Dock
21. Vivekananda Setu
22. Sir William Jones
23. Bankshall
24. Subhas Chandra Bose
25. Floatel

NostalgiCAL (A Mixed Bag)

1. Rudyard Kipling
2. Raja Ram Mohan Roy
3. To turn bullock carts into by-lanes, out of the way of the burra sahibs

4. Charlie Chaplin
5. Sambhunath Pandit
6. Napier of Magdalla
7. For fear of cholera
8. Rabindranath Tagore
9. Camac street
10. Music World
11. Michael Madhusudan Dutta
12. Meghnad Saha
13. Madras or Chennai
14. Prince Dwarkanath Tagore
15. Victoria Memorial
16. Yong Atchew. He is often regarded as the first Chinese settler in Bengal.
17. C.V. Raman
18. Banaphool
19. The Partition of Bengal
20. Raja Ram Mohan Roy
21. Peary Chand Mitra
22. Howrah Bridge
23. Prasanta Chandra Mahalanobis

24. Prafulla Chandra Ghosh
25. Acharya Jagadish Chandra Bose Indian Botanic Garden

PhysiCAL (Sports)

1. Chuni Goswami
2. Sujoy Ghosh
3. Mihir Sen
4. Bengal Warriors
5. S.S.P. Chawrasia
6. The Netaji Indoor Stadium
7. Table Tennis
8. Atlético de Kolkata
9. 1972
10. Rahul Banerjee and Dola Banerjee
11. Calcutta Cup
12. Dr Bidhan Chandra Roy
13. 'Gobor' Guha
14. Dibyendu Barua
15. Pancha Pandavas
16. Venezuela
17. Shyam Thapa

18. Norman Pritchard (in 1900 Paris Olympics, he won two silver medals)
19. Arjun Atwal
20. Sailen Manna
21. Pankaj Roy
22. Jagmohan Dalmiya
23. Saurav Ghosal
24. His brother Snehashish Ganguly
25. Leslie Claudius

RadiCAL (Milestones)

1. Rani Rashmoni
2. Jyoti Basu. The first cellular service of India was inaugurated in Calcutta on 31 July 1995.
3. U.N. Brahmachari
4. He was the first to marry a widow, a ten-year-old child, Kalimati.
5. Basanti Devi
6. Dr Jack Preger
7. Kazi Nazrul Islam
8. He is thought to be the first single man in India to father an in-vitro fertilized baby. The baby was born in 2005.

9. Steam engine
10. Mahasweta Devi
11. Swarnakumari Devi
12. Charu Mazumdar
13. Mahendra Lal Sircar
14. That Peak XV, later renamed Mount Everest, was the highest mountain in the world. He arrived at this conclusion after determining the height of Peak XV.
15. Alokananda Roy
16. Indian Association for the Cultivation of Science (IACS)
17. *Diana*
18. Hemendra Mohan Bose
19. Rashbehari Ghosh
20. Michael Madhusudan Dutta
21. Dinesh Gupta
22. Writer's Building
23. Bankim Chandra Chattopadhyay
24. That the Sun revolves around the Earth
25. Shiv Shankar Prasad Chawrasia

ReCAL (A Mixed Bag)

1. Dr Subhash Mukhopadhyay. The test tube baby, named

Kanupriya Agarwal alias Durga, was born on 3 October 1978. Since the government refused him recognition and did not allow him to attend international conferences, he committed suicide in his Calcutta residence.

2. Bhola Moira

3. Suchitra Mitra

4. He shot the first colour feature film, 'Ajit'. He received the President's award for 'Gotama the Buddha' (1956).

5. Sir William Jones

6. Rabindranath Tagore

7. Meghnad Saha

8. Over the Kalighat canal. On 1 June 1822, the bridge measuring 141 ft in length and 4 ft in width, was inaugurated.

9. Henry Derozio

10. Kadambini Ganguly and Chandramukhi Basu. They graduated in the 1880s. A hall in Calcutta University is named after them.

11. St John's Church

12. Surveyor General's office

13. Bagha Jatin

14. Diamond Harbour. The inaugural message was sent by Shiv Chunder Nandy, the first Indian in the Telegraph

Department.

15. Mahatma Gandhi Road (Harrison Road) in 1891
16. He was the first Jew to arrive in the city in 1798.
17. Ashapurna Devi
18. The Palki bearers. It was in demand of raising the fares which was eventually granted.
19. Raj Bhavan
20. On the boundary wall of SSKM Hospital
21. Upendranath Brahmachari. He was the first Indian to become the Chairman of the Managing Body of the Indian Red Cross Society of the Bengal Branch.
22. Matangini Hazra
23. GPO
24. Meghnad Saha
25. Sombhu Mitra

SabbatiCAL (Leisure)

1. Calcutta Club
2. Tolly Club
3. Calcutta South Club. Established in 1920.
4. Agricultural and Horticultural Society of India
5. Lord Curzon

6. The Lalit Great Eastern Hotel
7. The Park, Kolkata
8. The Saturday Club
9. The Royal Calcutta Golf Club
10. 1991
11. Calcutta International Club
12. Calcutta Club
13. Ecopark
14. Sir Charles Metcalfe
15. Kanika Bandopadhyay
16. Burdwan
17. Swabhumi
18. C.V. Raman
19. Science City
20. Aquatica
21. The Dalhousie Institute
22. Rabindra Sarobar
23. Zoological Garden, Alipore
24. Mani Square
25. Anderson Club

SymboliCAL (Customs and Traditions)

1. Simla Beyam Samity
2. The last 24 minutes of ashtami and the first 24 minutes of nabami make up the specific 'dudondo' (48 minutes) when Durga, as Chamunda, killed the demons Chanda and Munda. Shandhi Puja is performed at this point in time.
3. Mahalaya
4. *Jamai Sasthi.* It was a short film produced by Madan Theatres in 1931.
5. As Kolabou. These nine trees are rambha (banana/plantain), kachu (yam), haridra (turmeric), jayanti, bilva (wood apple or bel), darimba (pomegranate), ashok, maan (another variety of yam) and dhanya (paddy).
6. During Durga Puja in pre-independent India, the material for the decoration of the idol came from Germany by post and that is why it was called 'daker saaj'.
7. Years ago an accidental fire at the Kumortuli Puja damaged the images. Something had to be done. So the famous sculptor Gopeshwar Pal separated the images.
8. A child is initiated to write for the first time with chalk on Saraswati Puja day.
9. Kul or green plums
10. Tenacity

11. Bar Puja. The bar posts are worshipped in Calcutta Maidan.

12. Opening a new book of account by clearing all previous dues on Bengali New Year's day (Poila Boishakh).

13. It symbolized the progress of women.

14. Neelkantha pakhi (Indian Roller bird)

15. Axe and armour

16. Dakshineswar Temple

17. Maddox Square

18. Shitala Mata

19. Knowledge

20. Money

21. The first transaction of the day that is generally considered auspicious

22. Beneath the Howrah Bridge

23. Worship of Goddess Durga along with her children. It is Sabarna Roy Choudhury's family puja that started in 1610.

24. Settling down in a foreign land

25. On the day of Rath Yatra

TactiCAL (Administration)

1. Sergeant
2. Surendra Nath Chatterjee
3. A network of spies or goendas
4. The East India Company formally appointed an officer to be in charge of civil and criminal administration. He was assisted by an Indian functionary commonly known as a 'black deputy' or 'black zamindar'.
5. Sheriff
6. Warren Hastings
7. For having supervised this country's first ever general elections
8. He charged the funds to 'Road Improvement' because the title of the film was translated as *Song of the Road*
9. Fort William
10. Sir Stuart Hogg
11. Warren Hastings
12. Kolkata Police
13. The transfer of power from the Company Bahadur to the British Crown
14. Sabarna Roy Choudhury
15. Throne Room

16. Subhas Chandra Bose
17. Special Branch
18. Dr Rajendra Prasad
19. Purosree Bibardhan
20. Mounted Police
21. Sir Barnes Peacock
22. John Z. Holwell
23. Robert Clive
24. Padmaja Naidu
25. The entry of the Speaker into the House with a ceremonial procession headed by a Marshal bearing the Mace on his shoulder.

TheatriCAL (The Stage)

1. Sri Ramakrishna Paramahansa
2. Sans Souci Theatre
3. *Comedy of Errors*
4. Manoj Mitra's *Sajano Bagaan*
5. Shishir Kumar Bhaduri
6. *Nabanna*
7. Rabindranath Tagore
8. Ritwik Ghatak

9. Debabrata Biswas
10. *Angaar* in 1959 (for recreating flooded mines)
11. Nandikar
12. Badal Sircar (Born in 1925 as Sudhindranath Sircar)
13. Ajit Panja
14. Binodini Dasi
15. Sombhu Mitra
16. Girish Chandra Ghosh
17. Gerasim Lebedev
18. Utpal Dutt
19. Surendranath Ghosh
20. Michael Madhusudan Dutta
21. Debshankar Halder
22. Usha Ganguli
23. Tripti Mitra
24. Star Theatre
25. *Raktakarabi/Red Oleander*

TheologiCAL (Religion)

1. St Paul's Cathedral. Major William Nairn Forbes, with the assistance of C.K. Robinson designed the cathedral (completed in 1847), modelling the tower and spire upon

the Norwich Cathedral.

2. St John's Church

3. In the Chinese Kali Temple in China town (Around sixty years ago, local people worshipped a couple of sindoor-smeared black stones under an old tree. Seeing these stones, the Chinese started following suit and at this site the temple was established.

4. St Andrew's Church (The foundation stone was laid on St Andrew's Day)

5. Prince Ghulam Muhammad

6. Jora Girja

7. Swami Vivekananda

8. Toe

9. Shri Sheetalnathji, the 10th Jain Avtaar (It was built by an art connoisseur named Ray Badridas Bahadur in 1867)

10. Mithun Chakraborty

11. St Paul's Cathedral

12. Metcalfe Street or Bandook Gali

13. Rev. Alexander Duff

14. Chinese

15. Lake Kalibari

16. Mother Teresa

17. Akbar's mausoleum at Sikandra, Agra
18. Thanthania Kalibari
19. Kalighat pandas
20. Warren Hastings
21. Nichidatsu Fujii
22. Thomas Fanshawe Middleton
23. Lord Dalhousie
24. St John's Church
25. Birla Temple

VehiCAL (Transport)

1. Esplanade–Bhowanipore (now Netaji Bhavan)
2. French Motor Car Company Ltd
3. Prince Dwarkanath Tagore
4. Indira Gandhi. The Metro Railway project between Dum Dum and Tollygunge over a length of 16.45 km was sanctioned during 1972–73. The foundation stone of the project was laid by Indira Gandhi, the then Prime Minister of India, on 29 December 1972.
5. Blue
6. Banalata
7. Fire and Emergency Services

8. *Calcutta Mail*

9. Kundu Special

10. Kabi Nazrul Islam

11. Hooghly

12. *Do Bigha Zameen*

13. Swadeshi. Bepin Behari Das was a mechanic and worked in a small shed near Ballygunge Phari. Swadeshi was a 15hp L head 4-cylinder 5-seater and 4-door touring model car.

14. Keranchi-gari

15. Jibanananda Das

16. Shyambazar

17. Subhas Chandra Bose

18. Phaetons

19. Duronto Express

20. Behala Flying Club

21. Dhanbad

22. Smaranika

23. Chinese

24. Netaji Subhas Chandra Bose

25. Sealdah

VertiCAL (Buildings)

1. The Victorial Memorial
2. The Raj Bhavan or Governor's House
3. The Marble Palace
4. Peter Charles Earnest Paul
5. Messrs Martin & Co.
6. Writers' Building
7. Belgachia metro station
8. Metcalfe Hall
9. Fairlie Warehouse
10. The Gwalior Monument
11. The Calcutta High Court
12. Town Hall
13. The money for the construction of all of these structures was raised by means of lottery
14. Satyajit Ray
15. The Asiatic Society
16. Swami Vivekananda
17. *Nabanna*
18. Fort William

19. Charles Correa

20. Chatterjee International Centre

21. South City Mall

22. Egyptian

23. Hyderi Manzil

24. Subhas Chandra Bose

25. For making weather forecasts

VoCAL (Famous quotes)

1. Amitabh Bachchan

2. Mohammed Ali Jinnah to Lord Moutbatten in 1947, when it was decided that Bengal would be partitioned

3. Gunter Grass

4. Vidya Balan

5. Robert Clive

6. Amit Chaudhuri

7. Satyajit Ray

8. Edward Lear

9. Pele

10. Pranab Mukherjee

11. Gautam Gambhir

12. Rabindranath Tagore
13. *Kahaani*
14. Barack Obama
15. Winston Churchill
16. Mark Twain
17. Mrinal Sen, who filmed the city during a bandh
18. Vir Sanghvi
19. Sir George Trevelyan
20. V.S. Naipaul
21. Lenin
22. Basant Kumar Birla
23. Sunil Gavaskar
24. Shah Rukh Khan
25. Arati Mukherjee

Au revoir, Neil O'Brien

Ruskin Bond

Although Neil O'Brien had for long been a legend in the publishing and educational world, I met him for the first time in 2010, when we were both on the jury of a programme. Neil O'Brien and I hit it off almost immediately; we had so much in common—a love of literature, of history, of sports and we were the same age, which meant that there were memories to be shared and experiences recalled. I remember him telling me that his favourite film was *The Count of Monte Cristo,* which he had seen as a boy. We talked about all the famous books that had been filmed, something that seldom happens today, and the music of the 1930s and 40s.

He was India's first quizmaster and his wide knowledge of world affairs, past and present, gave him the edge when interviewing students. After this, we met on several occasions. He even took me home and gave me my favourite Anglo-Indian dish: ball curry. I look forward to meeting him in the Great Beyond and maybe there we can watch *The Count of Monte Cristo* together.

www.ingramcontent.com/pod-product-compliance
Lightning Source LLC
La Vergne TN
LVHW090951080826
845145LV00003B/969

* 9 7 8 8 1 2 9 1 3 6 6 4 0 *